"By myself have I sworn," saith the Lord,

"...That in blessing I will bless thee,

and in multiplying I will multiply

thy seed as the stars of the heaven..."

Genesis 22:16-17 (KJV)

Seven Keys to Hundredfold Blessings

Unlocking the Abraham Promise

Berin Gilfillan

Published by:

Powerhouse Publishing

PO Box 99, Fawnskin CA 92333

www.powerhousepublishing.org

(909) 866 3119

Second Edition

Printed in USA

Contents

Foreword

Berin Gilfillan and *The International School of Ministry*
(ISOM) are in the center of God's end-time plan for the nations.
The powerful book you are holding contains the teaching at the
core of their vision.

God's promise to Abraham is the bedrock of our history with
God, a spiritual "promissory note" to His children throughout
the ages. By faith, we share in His great covenant promises
of fruitfulness, blessings, and victory spoken to Abraham
thousands of years ago!

That's why this book is so important. Our lives are their
richest when we understand and appropriate the divine
provisions God made available through the Abrahamic
covenant; and we are fulfilled when the nations are blessed
through us, as God foretold.

Reading these pages, you will gain a deeper understanding of
who you are...and the importance of your place in the world,
as God's powerful promise and hundredfold blessing to *you* are
unlocked!

Dr. Marilyn Hickey – January 2004

Dedication

This book is dedicated to those who labor for Christ on the front lines of ministry all over the world. Especially included are those who translate God's Word and ministry materials into the languages and dialects of unreached peoples. Also to be honored are missionaries who step out of their comfort zones and risk all to bring the gospel to people who have not yet heard the saving message of the cross. Finally, this book is dedicated to pastors all over the planet who passionately and faithfully shepherd God's people. All these folks are God's heros. They will get the largest crowns in heaven and the greatest rewards for all eternity. May God bless them through this book and may He encourage them in the critical Kingdom work that they do.

Praying the Abraham Promise

Lord, I thank You that I am the seed of Abraham because I belong to Christ Jesus. I am therefore an heir of the promise that You swore to Abraham. I ask that blessing You will bless me, and multiplying, You will multiply me as the stars in the heaven and the sand on the seashore. I ask that I will possess the gate of my enemies, and that through Christ in me, all the nations of the earth will be blessed.

Introduction

This book has been like an unborn child, where the pregnancy has gone far past full term. If this child does not get born, it will cause great discomfort to the one carrying it. In the pages that follow, a bold vision and plan for the Christian church around the world is presented. The body of Christ desperately needs to understand the powerful truths contained in the Abraham promise. Locked in it are secrets both eternal and global in their significance. Hopefully, through this book, you will begin to partake of the incredible benefits contained in the promise to Abraham.

In the past seven years, I have applied the principles outlined in this book to the front lines of ministry around the world. Using the concepts you are about to learn, God has helped our ministry create a tangible tool for the body of Christ. It is called the International School of Ministry, or ISOM for short. The ISOM consists of 160 hours of video training material from over 30 outstanding international instructors. It is a bilingual video Bible school designed to turn any church in the world into a ministry training center. Some have dubbed this program "the training equivalent of the *Jesus* film." For those not familiar with the *Jesus* film, it is an evangelism movie developed by an organization called Campus Crusade for Christ. The film is a powerful depiction of the life of Christ based on the book of

Luke. It currently is available in hundreds of languages and is used in many nations to clearly present the life and message of Jesus.

Bringing people to a saving knowledge of Christ is only the first step in the Christian walk. What has been requested for years by missionaries and Christian workers, is a teaching and discipleship tool with the same translation capability as the *Jesus* film. The ISOM is helping to meet this huge need. In its first seven years, the ISOM has enabled over 10,000 video Bible training schools to start. These schools began in eighty-four countries and in over sixty of the world's major languages. Currently, at least 100,000 believers are being prepared for ministry through the ISOM program. There is every indication that millions more will follow.

The principles I am about to share are working in an extraordinary way for the ISOM project, but I am convinced they can be applied to any life or ministry. The health and strength of what is happening through the ISOM have simply added fuel to the strong prompting in my spirit to get into print the biblical foundations undergirding our vision. Although I use the ISOM program as a practical illustration throughout the book, the purpose is not to create a literary commercial for the program. The ISOM is one tool out of many and simply provides a prototype. When the principles are followed, practical models can be created by anyone to unlock the Abraham promise.

The target audience of this book is end-time harvest saints. The initial pages will stir in believers a sense of potential and help them catch a greater vision for their lives. As the book progresses, the material will speak more to those aspiring to leadership, those who want to help build God's kingdom and reap the end-time harvest.

Even if you are not on the frontlines of public ministry, this book will help you. If a subject does not seem to apply to you, don't discard it. Use those areas to give you an understanding of how to pray for Christian leaders and how to intercede for the advancement of Christ's kingdom in these critical days of history. It is my prayer that as you read these pages, revelation will come and God will make you fruitful and multiply you as the stars in the heaven.

Chapter 1
The Abraham Promise

In recent years, the prayer of Jabez has blessed millions of people. Although the secrets contained in this prayer had been tucked away in God's Word for generations, a modern-day revelation of that prayer has unlocked wonderful blessings for believers around the world. The promise to Abraham in Genesis

> *"... you will discover that you are a co-inheritor with Abraham of a huge, God-ordained promissory note."*

22 is another hidden treasure waiting to be discovered. It is so significant that God's end-time plan for the earth may well rest on the church understanding it. In the pages that follow, you will receive some keys to unlocking its treasures.

Let's take a close look at the Abraham promise. In this Scripture, Abraham had just placed his son Isaac on an altar and raised a knife to kill his beloved child. Then God made an incredible promise.

"By myself have I sworn," saith the Lord, "for because thou hast done this thing, and hast not withheld thy son, thine only son: That in blessing I will bless thee, and in multiplying I will multiply thy seed as the stars of the heaven, and as the sand

which is upon the sea shore; and thy seed shall possess the gate
of his enemies; And in thy seed shall all the nations of the earth
be blessed; because thou hast obeyed my voice."
Genesis 22:16-18 (KJV)

When a person wins a modern-day lottery worth millions
of dollars, others enviously watch their joyful response on
television. They imagine what it might be like if they ever
were so fortunate. It is easy to be impressed by the winnings
of others. But imagine what it would be like if you discovered,
while watching another winner, that you were a co-winner, that
the numbers on your ticket also matched the winning numbers
being announced. Immediately, your joy would be greatly
increased. This is because you would be a beneficiary. Suddenly,
in a real sense, riches beyond your wildest dreams would be in
the pipeline to you. At the point of discovering the news, you
would not have one penny of the money. Your key to those
riches would lie in understanding how to redeem your winning
ticket.

In the pages ahead, you will discover that you are a co-
inheritor with Abraham of a huge, God-ordained promissory
note.

Chapter 2
Who Is Abraham's Seed?

Specifically, the target of the Abraham promise of blessing and multiplication is given to the seed of Abraham. Let's look at a key part of this promise.

*"That in blessing I will bless thee, and in multiplying I will multiply thy **seed** as the stars of the heaven, And in thy **seed** shall all the nations of the earth be blessed.*
***Genesis 22:16-18** (KJV) (emphasis added)*

The Hebrew word for "seed" in these verses is *zera'* (zeh'-rah). This word is translated as "seed, child, fruitful, sowing time and seedtime."[1] In this context, the Hebrew word is definitely referring to "child." The New Testament throws more light on this scriptural promise. Let's see what Paul wrote to the Galatians about this verse.

> *"... when it comes to being the seed of Abraham, no discrimination is allowed."*

*Now to Abraham and his **seed** were the promises made. He saith not, And to seeds, as of many; but as of one, And to thy **seed**, which is Christ. **Galatians 3:16** (KJV) (emphasis added)*

I like the way the Living Bible brings out what Paul meant.

Now, God gave some promises to Abraham and his Child. And notice that it doesn't say the promises were to his children, as it would if all his sons—all the Jews—were being spoken of, but to his Child—and that, of course, means Christ. (TLB)

A few verses later, Paul sheds more light on who the seed of Abraham really is:

*For you are all sons of God through faith in Christ Jesus. For as many of you as were baptized into Christ have put on Christ. There is neither Jew nor Greek, there is neither slave nor free, there is neither male nor female; for you are all one in Christ Jesus. And if you are Christ's, then **you are Abraham's seed**, and **heirs according to the promise**. Galatians 3:26-29 (emphasis added)*

ESSENTIAL CONCEPT #1: If you are a believer in Jesus Christ, and if you are a practicing Christian, *you* are an inheritor of this awesome Abraham promise.

God actually swears this oath by Himself, the highest form of oath possible in heaven or earth. The writer of the book of Hebrews explains how this oath was given;

For when God made a promise to Abraham, because He could swear by no one greater, He swore by Himself, saying, "Surely blessing I will bless you, and multiplying I will multiply you." And so, after he had patiently endured, he obtained the promise. Hebrews 6:13-15

The writer of Hebrews discusses the significance of this oath. The Living Bible puts it this way.

When a man takes an oath, he is calling upon someone greater than himself to force him to do what he has promised or to punish him if he later refuses to do it; the oath ends all argument about it. God also bound himself with an oath, so that those He promised to help would be perfectly sure and never need to wonder whether He might change His plans. He has given us both His promise and His oath, two things we can completely count on, for it is impossible for God to tell a lie. Now all those who flee to Him to save them can take new courage when they hear such assurances from God.
Hebrews 6:16-18 (TLB)

ESSENTIAL CONCEPT #2: The second critical point to the Abraham promise is that, when it comes to being the seed of Abraham, *no discrimination* is allowed.

Let's go back to the book of Galatians and look more closely at verse 28;

There is neither Jew nor Greek, there is neither slave nor free, there is neither male nor female; for you are all one in Christ Jesus. **Galatians 3:28**

Being the seed of Abraham transcends the issue of race (neither Jew nor Greek, neither black or white, neither yellow or brown). It also transcends the issue of class (neither slave nor free, rich or poor, educated or uneducated,) and finally,

it precludes gender discrimination (neither male nor female).
No matter what your race, economic or social background,
or gender, this promise to Abraham belongs to all believing
Christians.

Fruitfulness, Blessings, & Victory Waiting to be Unlocked

Let me briefly summarize. There is a promise in the Scriptures
that is available to *all* Christians, male and female, of *all* races
and economic backgrounds. The promise will bring about
massive fruitfulness and blessings in the lives of *all* believers. It
guarantees triumphant living over *all* one's enemies and opens
up nation-reaching and nation-blessing potential. It is backed by
the highest oath in the universe, and it is waiting to be unlocked.
Hold on to your seats. In the chapters ahead you will discover
how to unlock and release this awesome promise into your life.

Chapter 3
I Will Multiply
Your Seed

In order to unlock the Abraham promise, we must delve deeply into its wording. In Genesis 1, God gave Adam and Eve a blessing and a commandment but He did not make them a promise. Let's look at that blessing and commandment.

*So God created man in His own image; in the image of God He created him; male and female He created them. Then God blessed them, and God said to them, "Be fruitful and multiply; fill the earth and subdue it; have dominion over the fish of the sea, over the birds of the air, and over every living thing that moves on the earth." **Genesis 1:27-28***

Although God used the word *multiply*, it is clear from this verse that the primary responsibility for the accomplishment of this commandment is in the hands of Adam and Eve and their descendants. Fortunately for us, being fruitful and multiplying is the one commandment that men and women from

"... Dr. Simon Driver, commented, "Even for a professional astronomer used to dealing in monster numbers, this is mind-boggling."

the beginning of time have been very successful at keeping. With over six billion souls now on the planet, mankind is definitely making strides toward filling the earth. The huge difference between the "multiply" in Genesis 1 and the "multiply" in Genesis 22 is *who* is doing the multiplying.

In Genesis 1, Adam and Eve, mankind, was given the responsibility to multiply. In Genesis 22, God is the one who does the multiplying. This has major implications with regard to our study of the Abraham promise.

Why are Christians Not Multiplying?

When I was pondering this Scripture while a student at Fuller Theological Seminary in Pasadena, California, this seemingly small issue of who was doing the multiplying troubled me. My question to God was, "Why are Christians not multiplying and why is the church around the world not growing in significant numbers?" The statistics I was studying showed that the church in most parts of the world was barely keeping pace with population growth. In the Gospels, Jesus took five loaves and two small fish and in a matter of minutes multiplied them to feed close to 20,000 people (5,000 men plus women and children - Matthew 14:21).

In the Old Testament, the children of Israel questioned whether God could supply meat in the wilderness for over two million people. God was not happy with their doubt. Not as a blessing, but as a demonstration of His power, God dumped quail on Israel in abundance. I am not sure people have quite grasped just HOW MANY BIRDS God provided. Let's look at that Scripture.

Now a wind went out from the Lord and drove quail in from the sea. It brought them down all around the camp to about three feet above the ground, as far as a day's walk in any direction. **Numbers 11:31 (NIV)**

Imagine a pile of quail 3 feet high for 24 miles in every direction. That is a lot of birds! God proved His point. He surely is able to MULTIPLY.

The Stars in the Heaven

Getting back to the Abraham promise, we see God using the examples of the immeasurable stars in the heaven and grains of sand on the seashore.

I recently read about a study done by some Australian astronomers[2]. They did a calculation to determine the number of stars in the known universe. They came up with 70 sextillion; that is 7 followed by 22 zeros, or 70 thousand million million million. To give you something earthly to compare this number with, there are about ten times as many stars as there are grains of sand on all the world's beaches and deserts. That is a lot of stars.

The research was actually done by a team of stargazers from the Australian National University. They took a single strip in the heavens, calculated the stars in that one section, and then multiplied it out to cover the entire sky. This was surely easier than counting every single star. The one strip chosen contained about 10,000 galaxies. The number of stars in each galaxy was determined by a careful measurement of the brightness of each galaxy.

These findings were released in 2003 at the General Assembly of the International Astronomical Union in Sydney, Australia. The figures presented were said to be ten times more accurate than any previous calculation. The leader of the stargazing team, Dr. Simon Driver, commented, "Even for a professional astronomer used to dealing in monster numbers, this is mind-boggling." He added that this is the number of stars in the observable universe, using some of the most powerful telescopes currently available. He said the true number could actually be infinite.

That is the kind of multiplication God wants to do in your life– like the stars in the heaven and the sand on the seashore. The nagging question still remains: "If God is able to multiply the seed of Abraham like the stars in the heaven, and He has promised to do so, why then are God's people NOT multiplying?"

Man's Part Versus God's Part

God is never at fault when His people are not enjoying some benefit promised in Scripture. The fault is always on the side of fallible humans and so I began to search God's Word for the answer. The first clue into this mystery of unlocking the multiplication contained in the Abraham promise came from this very short verse found in Paul's letter to the Corinthians.

I planted, Apollos watered, but God gave the increase.
1 Corinthians 3:6

Even though I had read this verse in Corinthians many times, I became suddenly aware of an equation in these few words. Paul writes, "I planted" - that is a human function. Then "Apollos watered" - another human function. Finally, God gave the increase - a Divine function. If we put this into a crude mathematical equation we get:

I planted (human function)
> **+ Apollos watered (human function)**
>> **= God's increase (multiplication growth)**

When I saw this simple equation, I became very excited. I realized that God's multiplication is only in response to man specifically planting and watering. If man does not do his part, the multiplication of God will never happen.

My next search was to discover what the Scriptures specifically revealed concerning what man's part and what God's part is pertaining to multiplication growth. In the following pages, I will unfold seven areas that God has promised to multiply if the church and individual Christians will do their part.

Chapter 4
Word Multiplication

Key #1 – God Will Multiply His Word
if Believers Sow God's Word

At the core of God's multiplication principles lies His
Word. Discovering its secrets and its multiplication potential
is critical to unlocking the Abraham promise. A key Bible
passage describing multiplication in God's kingdom and the
multiplication of
God's Word is
Matthew 13. It starts
with the parable of
the sower. Let's take a
closer look;

> *"... A hundred-fold return is a
> 10,000 percent multiplication of the
> original seed. If you told a Wall Street
> stockbroker you could get that type of
> return, you would have his interest."*

Then He spoke many things to them in parables, saying:
"Behold, a sower went out to sow. And as he sowed, some seed
fell by the wayside; and the birds came and devoured them.
Some fell on stony places, where they did not have much earth;
and they immediately sprang up because they had no depth
of earth. But when the sun was up they were scorched, and
because they had no root they withered away. And some fell
among thorns, and the thorns sprang up and choked them.

*But others fell on good ground and yielded a crop: some a
hundredfold, some sixty, some thirty. He who has ears to hear,
let him hear!" **Matthew 13:3-9***

From verses 18 to 23, Christ explains clearly to His disciples
the meaning of the parable of the sower.

*Therefore hear the parable of the sower: When anyone hears
the word of the Kingdom, and does not understand it, then
the wicked one comes and snatches away what was sown in
his heart. This is he who received seed by the wayside. But he
who received the seed on stony places, this is he who hears the
word and immediately receives it with joy; Yet he has no root
in himself, but endures only for a while. For when tribulation
or persecution arises because of the word, immediately he
stumbles. Now he who received seed among the thorns is he who
hears the word, and the cares of this world and the deceitfulness
of riches choke the word, and he becomes unfruitful. But he who
received seed on the good ground is he who hears the word and
understands it, who indeed bears fruit and produces: some a
hundredfold, some sixty, some thirty. **Matthew 13:18-23***

This is one of the most obvious and clear illustrations in God's
Word of seed, sowing and multiplication growth. The parable
of the sower unlocks so many mysteries that Jesus said the
following about it in Mark 4:13.

*"Do you not understand this parable? How then will you
understand all the parables?" **Mark 4:13***

Divine Seeds

For the purposes of this book, we need to understand the tremendous latent power contained in a seed. The words of God are divine seeds. People seldom understand the enormous growth and multiplication potential that can be unleashed when they sow that seed into their hearts or when they sow that seed into the hearts of others. Nearly all the forms of multiplication we will study are directly tied to the sowing of God's Word.

The parable of the sower contains three distinct parts. Human beings are the sowers. The target is the hearts of people, and the seed is God's Word. Seed landing on a good heart can yield a thirty, sixty or a hundred-fold return. A hundred-fold return is a 10,000 percent multiplication of the original seed. If you told a Wall Street stockbroker you could get that type of return, you would have his interest. So how can believers unlock the power of multiplication through the sowing of God's Word?

This principle of the multiplication of God's Word pertains to sowing into the hearts of believers and non-believers alike. Sowing the initial seed of salvation through the proclamation of the gospel is what Paul talked about in 1 Corinthians 1:21.

For since, in the wisdom of God, the world through wisdom did not know God, it pleased God through the foolishness of the message preached to save those who believe.
1 Corinthians 1:21

> *"... The preaching of the Cross is the detonator of multiplication growth in the life of a believer."*

The Word of God – A Detonator of Multiplication Growth

The Word of God has the power to eternally save a human soul when faith to believe the gospel is imparted by preaching. This is what the apostle Paul was referring to when he said, "I planted." He was speaking about the simple proclamation of the Cross and the power of believing in what Christ has done by dying for the world. His words in 1 Corinthians 2:1-2 leave no doubt what he meant when he spoke of the initial planting of the message of the Cross and salvation into the lives of people in the Corinthian church.

1 Corinthians 2:1-2 And I, brethren, when I came to you, did not come with excellence of speech or of wisdom declaring to you the testimony of God. For I determined not to know anything among you except Jesus Christ and Him crucified.

A little earlier, in 1 Corinthians 1:18, Paul wrote:

For the message of the cross is foolishness to those who are perishing, but to us who are being saved it is the power of God.
1 Corinthians 1:18

The preaching of the Cross is the detonator of multiplication growth in the life of a believer. There is no other message that releases the power of God in a person's life and causes the human spirit to be born again and to become a new creation with God's life within it. This is the incorruptible seed spoken about by the apostle Peter.

Having been born again, not of corruptible seed but incorruptible, through the word of God which lives and abides forever. **1 Peter 1:23**

God's Word – The Devil's Target

It is no wonder that the devil fights the initial sowing of the seed of God's Word into people's hearts. In the parable of the sower, the attacks of the enemy are not against individuals. They are targeted against the seed of God's Word. Let's take a closer look at the ways the devil tries to stop the Word.

1) Seed by the wayside. The devil steals <u>the Word</u> away because it is not understood.

2) Seed on stony places. Tribulation and persecution destroy <u>the Word</u> when the heart does not allow it to root deeply.

3) Seed among thorns. The cares of the world and deceitfulness of riches chokes <u>the Word</u>. The result is that <u>the Word</u> does not bear fruit.

The parable of the sower has powerful implications when it comes to the development of the seed from the point of entering the human heart into the place of maturity and ultimately to a 30-, 60- or 100-fold return.

The Word of God not only enables the initial miracle of salvation to transpire, it has the power to water that seed and radically transform a believer's life into the image of Christ. This process causes the grain of wheat to die and then become a seed of multiplication. Jesus said in John 12:24:

*"Most assuredly, I say to you, unless a grain of wheat falls into the ground and dies, it remains alone; but if it dies, it produces much grain." **John 12:24***

We will look at the watering of the planted seed in the next chapter. In Chapter 11, "Conquering the Sin Nature", we will look in depth at the death and resurrection of that grain of wheat in our lives.

Chapter 5
The Role of the Teacher in Watering God's Seed

The Bible says that man shall not live by bread alone but by every Word that proceeds from the mouth of the Lord (Deuteronomy 8:3). The Scriptures are able to impart life-giving sustenance to a believer, but they also contain a major key in bringing about the multiplication growth promised to Abraham. The following observation may surprise some.

The most powerful ministerial office for watering the initial seed of salvation to full multiplication in a believer's life is that of the teacher. Let's look again at what Paul wrote in 1 Corinthians 3:6;

> *"... The most powerful ministerial office for watering the initial seed of salvation to full multiplication in a believer's life is that of the teacher."*

I planted, Apollos watered, but God gave the increase.
1 Corinthians 3:6

Apollos watered the seed Paul planted before God gave the increase. Apollos was a teacher. Let's take a closer look at his ministry:

*Now a certain Jew named Apollos, born at Alexandria, an eloquent man and mighty in the Scriptures, came to Ephesus. This man had been instructed in the way of the Lord; and being fervent in spirit, he spoke and **taught accurately** the things of the Lord. Acts 18:23-24 (emphasis added)*

When a natural seed is planted, it is an instantaneous event. The watering of a seed, however, is a critical process that takes time and diligence. Lack of moisture can kill a young plant before it gets a chance to bear fruit. As in the natural, so it is in the spiritual.

Apollos was *"mighty in the Scriptures"* and he had been *"instructed in the way of the Lord."* The seed of God's Word began to multiply as he *"spoke and taught accurately the things of the Lord."*

Acts 18:27 states that when Apollos went to Corinth he "greatly helped those who had believed through grace; for he vigorously refuted the Jews publicly, showing from the Scriptures that Jesus is the Christ."

The Power of the Teacher –
Making God's Word Understandable

About five centuries before Christ[3], when the nation of Israel was returning from its captivity in Persia, God prepared a man who would be instrumental in reestablishing the spiritual foundations of the Hebrew nation. His name was Ezra and he was a teacher. This is what the Bible says about him.

*For Ezra had prepared his heart to seek the Law of the Lord, and to
do it, and to **teach** statutes and ordinances in Israel.*
Ezra 7:10 *(emphasis added)*

What is it about the role of the teacher that is so critical in
causing the seed of salvation in a human heart to come to a place
of multiplication? It starts with the ability of a teacher to make
God's Word **understandable**. Remember when we mentioned
the parable of the sower and the different ways the devil tries to
stop God's Word. Let's look at that Scripture a little closer;

*Therefore hear the parable of the sower: When anyone hears
the word of the Kingdom, and **does not understand it**, then
the wicked one comes and snatches away what was sown in his
heart. This is he who received seed by the wayside.*
Matthew 13:18-19 *(emphasis added)*

When a person does not understand God's Word, the devil is
able to steal it. When a person does understand it, let's see what
happens;

*But he who received seed on the good ground is he who hears the
word and **understands** it, who indeed bears fruit and produces:
some a hundredfold, some sixty, some thirty.*
Matthew 13:23 *(emphasis added)*

Now, let us look closer at the life and ministry of Ezra, and
at those who came with him to Jerusalem to establish again the
spiritual foundations of the nation.

*So Ezra the priest brought the Law before the assembly of men and women and all who could hear **with understanding** on the first day of the seventh month. Then he read from it in the open square that was in front of the Water Gate from morning until midday, before the men and women and those who **could understand**; and the ears of all the people were attentive to the Book of the Law **Nehemiah 8:2-3** (emphasis added)*

*Also Jeshua,...Pelaiah, and the Levites, helped the people **to understand** the Law; and the people stood in their place. So they read distinctly from the book, in the Law of God; and they gave the sense, and **helped them to understand** the reading. **Nehemiah 8:7-8** (emphasis added)*

Again and again, God's Word emphasizes the necessity of making the Law understandable to people. This is where the gift of the teacher comes in.

I am a great fan of Gideon's International, the organization that distributes the Gideon Bible. They have filled most hotel and motel rooms on the planet with Bibles in the nightstands. It is ironic that some of the worst sins on the planet take place in those hotel and motel rooms. The availability of God's Word does not bring about life transformation. Only the expounding of God's Word in a way that brings revelation can change lives. God expects parents and leaders to do this with the younger generation.

You shall love the Lord your God with all your heart, with all your soul and with all your strength. And these words which

*I command you today shall be in your heart.***You shall teach them** *diligently to your children and shall talk of them when you sit in your house, when you walk by the way, when you lie down and when you rise up.* **Deuteronomy 6:5-7** *(emphasis added)*

When teaching is not done well, the Word of God becomes dull and boring. That is why there is a need for people with great communication skills. Most of all, teachers need a powerful touch of the Holy Spirit on their lives. That touch from God is what made the teachings of Jesus have so much impact. One of the greatest examples of Jesus teaching and opening His Word to His disciples can be found in Luke 24:27-32. This discourse took place after Jesus rose from the dead on the Emmaus road:

And beginning at Moses and all the Prophets, He expounded to them in all the Scriptures the things concerning Himself. **Luke 24:27**

Then their eyes were opened and they knew Him; and He vanished from their sight. **And they said to one another, "Did not our heart burn within us while He talked with us on the road, and while He opened the Scriptures to us?"** **Luke 24:31-32** *(emphasis added)*

> "... The availability of God's Word does not bring about life transformation. Only the expounding of God's Word in a way that brings revelation can change lives."

Jesus brought God's Word alive to His disciples. As He opened their understanding, they felt God's Spirit burning the truth of the Word into their hearts. This is the kind of dynamic teaching that is needed in the church today. Teachers must impart understanding in such a way that it ignites the hearts of the hearers and illuminates their minds with truth from the Scriptures.

Teaching Through Example

The teaching of God's Word needs to go beyond a dynamic impartation of knowledge. It should also involve lifestyle and example. Paul wrote to Timothy:

But you have carefully followed my doctrine, manner of life, purpose, faith, longsuffering, love, perseverance.
2 Timothy 3:10

Spiritual training involves the totality of a person's way of life. The old adage used by many parents, "Do what I say and not what I do," holds no water with today's generation. I was amused to hear the following story of the great spiritual leader of India, Mahatma Gandhi[4]. Though he was not a Christian, he taught many good principles about life that are worth following.

A worried mother had an elementary-age boy who ate large amounts sweets whenever she was not looking. She tried to hide the candy but the boy always found it. He also got candy from relatives and neighbors. His mother told him often how bad the candy was for him and how it would destroy his teeth and his health but the boy would not listen. Finally she took him to see the famous Mahatma Gandhi.

Gandhi was a living legend, highly respected in all of India at that time. The mother knew if Gandhi told the boy to stop eating candy, he would certainly listen. After three days of standing in a long line to get an audience with the great leader, she told him her problem. "Please," she begged, "will you tell my son to stop eating candy. I know he will obey you."

> *"... The teaching of God's Word needs to go beyond a dynamic impartation of knowledge. It should also involve lifestyle and example."*

Mr. Gandhi quietly said, "please come back and see me in two weeks."

The mother left with her son, not understanding why they had to come back after waiting three days in line. But she did not dare question the wisdom of this revered man.

Two weeks later, after waiting three more days in the long line to get another audience with Mahatma Gandhi, she brought her boy to the great leader and again presented her request.

Gandhi looked at the young boy sternly. "Young man, I want you to stop eating candy."

The boy looked wide eyed at the great leader, then bowed down and said, "Yes, sir. I will not eat candy anymore."

As the mother and son were leaving, she turned back. "Mr. Gandhi, sir," she said, "why did I need to wait in that long line a second time? Why did you not tell my son to stop eating candy two weeks ago?"

Gandhi looked at the woman with a twinkle in his eye, "it took me that long to stop eating candy myself."

Chapter 6
Teaching to Triumph Over All Enemies

The principle of accurately teaching the Scriptures in word and deed has another dimension. A critical part of the Abraham promise involves possessing the gate of our enemies. In the Old Testament the gates of a city were the places where decisions were made. Whoever possessed the gates had the power of decision making in that city.

In a modern context, possessing the gates means that people get to dominate over the fate of their enemies. When people unlock this part of the Abraham promise, they come to a place where they can live victoriously over the attacks of the devil.

There is an amazing connection in God's Word between people being taught the Scriptures and having victory over both natural and spiritual enemies. It is tragic that when the Jewish nation went astray, it was often because a generation dropped the ball in the area of

> *"... There is an amazing connection in God's Word between people being taught the Scriptures and having victory over both natural and spiritual enemies."*

teaching its children. What resulted was an ignorance of God's standards and His promises. This led to people deserting God's paths, going their own way, and suffering defeat at the hands of their enemies.

When King Asa took the throne of Judah, the nation had strayed far from its godly moorings. King Asa was a good man and he set his heart to seek God. The Lord sent the prophet Azariah to him and spoke the following word.

And he went out to meet Asa, and said to him: "Hear me, Asa, and all Judah and Benjamin. The Lord is with you while you are with Him. If you seek Him, He will be found by you; but if you forsake Him, He will forsake you. For a long time Israel has been without the true God, without a teaching priest, and without law." **2 Chronicles 15:2-3**

God attributed the nation's spiritual demise to not having a teaching priest. Since the Jews did not have knowledge of the Scriptures, they stopped seeking God and ended up being forsaken by the Lord.

Jehoshaphat's Key to Victory – Teaching God's Word to Judah

Another dramatic example of this principle in the Bible is in the life and kingdom of Jehoshophat. He realized the value of instruction and teaching early on in his reign, and he invested massively in teaching the nation God's Word.

Also in the third year of his reign he (Jehoshophat) sent
his leaders, Ben-Hail, Obadiah, Zechariah, Nethanel, and
Michaiah, **to teach** *in the cities of Judah. And with them he*
sent Levites: Shemaiah,... and Tobadonijah– the Levites; and
with them Elishama and Jehoram, the priests. So they **taught** *in*
Judah, and had the Book of the Law of the Lord with them; they
went throughout **all** *the cities of Judah and* **taught** *the people.*
2 Chronicles 17:7-9 *(emphasis added)*

The result of this emphasis on teaching was immediately
evident. Jehoshaphat's strategy helped the nation unlock that
key part of the Abraham promise: **triumphant living over**
their enemies. This started with a fear of God falling upon the
surrounding nations.

And the fear of the Lord fell on all the kingdoms of the lands
that were around Judah, so that they did not make war
against Jehoshophat. **2 Chronicles 17:10**

When the inhabitants of a nation are taught the knowledge
of God, the result is a positive impact on the psychological
well-being of the people. There is also a tangible change in the
spiritual atmosphere around them. As God's children come to
know their covenant promises, they learn to place their trust in
the Most High. It is then that the demonic world and the secular
world begin to have a new respect for God's people.

Jehoshaphat invested in teaching God's Word to the people.
He not only did this in large, prominent cities, he also had three
levels of leadership traveling throughout <u>all</u> the cities of Judah

to <u>teach</u> the people. These were his elders, his priests, and his Levites. Later in his reign, he became personally involved in this process. Notice in the following Scripture the use of the term "chief fathers" to describe some of these teaching elders.

So Jehoshaphat dwelt at Jerusalem; and he went out again among the people from Beersheba to the mountains of Ephraim, and brought them back to the Lord God of their fathers.
2 Chronicles 19:4

Moreover in Jerusalem, for the judgment of the Lord and for controversies, Jehoshaphat appointed some of the Levites and priests, and some of the chief fathers of Israel, when they returned to Jerusalem. **2 Chronicles 19:8**

We today need "chief fathers" who will trouble themselves to go out into less-known towns, teaching people and bringing them back to a rich faith in God. We need leaders who set an example and are willing to invest in the biblical instruction of God's people.

The most fascinating part of the story of Jehoshaphat is what happened following these events, when a massive army attacked his kingdom.

It happened after this that the people of Moab with the people of Ammon, and others with them besides the Ammonites, came to battle against Jehoshaphat. Then some came and told Jehoshaphat, saying, "A great multitude is coming against you from beyond the sea, from Syria; and they are in Hazazon Tamar" (which is En Gedi). And Jehoshaphat feared, and set *himself to seek the Lord, and proclaimed a fast throughout all Judah. So Judah gathered together to ask help from the Lord; and from **all the cities of Judah** they came to seek the Lord.* **2 Chronicles 20:1-4** *(emphasis added)*

Jehoshaphat had <u>taught</u> a nation to know God and trust in Him. I have heard many times that the secret to Jehoshaphat's victory was the singers and dancers who went ahead of his army. I beg to disagree with this conclusion. I believe his victory was won because he <u>taught</u> a nation to trust in God.

> *"... The singers and dancers were simply the mop-up crew to celebrate and usher in the victory."*

When trouble came, the whole nation gathered to seek help from the Lord. They knew God could help them because they had been <u>taught</u> His Word and His ways. God's promise to Abraham of victory over their enemies suddenly became a reality to them. Let's look at how Jehoshaphat prayed.

"O, our God, will You not judge them? For we have no power against this great multitude that is coming against us; nor do we know what to do, but our eyes are upon You." Now all Judah, with their little ones, their wives, and their children, stood before the Lord. **2 Chronicles 20:12-13**

What a poignant scene. A nation gathered in humility before their Creator - whole families with their eyes and hearts firmly set upon their God. Years of seeding God's Word into a nation had taught them to fear, love, trust, and obey the Lord. It is no wonder that God spoke prophetically into this situation.

*Then the Spirit of the Lord came upon Jahaziel the son of Zechariah, the son of Benaiah, the son of Jeiel, the son of Mattaniah, a Levite of the sons of Asaph, in the midst of the assembly. And he said, "Listen, all you of Judah and you inhabitants of Jerusalem, and you, King Jehoshaphat! Thus says the Lord to you: 'Do not be afraid nor dismayed because of this great multitude, for the battle is not yours, but God's...'You will not need to fight in this battle. Position yourselves, stand still and see the salvation of the Lord, who is with you, O Judah and Jerusalem!' Do not fear or be dismayed; tomorrow go out against them, for the Lord is with you." **2 Chronicles 20:14-15**

When God spoke this prophetic word, the battle was already won. The singers and dancers were simply the mop-up crew to celebrate and usher in the victory.

When God showed me this key of teaching contained in the Jehoshaphat story, I became very excited. These are powerful revelations that can be directly applied to our day and to reaching and teaching people for Christ. Through proliferating teaching to the far corners of his nation, Jehoshaphat was able to change the destiny of his people. Through a similar approach, we can help change the destiny of many in our generation.

What does this say to the church today? If we want to unlock the Abraham promise, we must open our lives wider to solid teaching ministries. So much of the outreach focus in the church has been on big crusades and on using other literature and media evangelism tools. We need now to develop teaching tools, because those will bring long-term fruit. As Solomon wisely counseled his son:

*Take firm hold of **instruction**, do not let go; keep her, for she is your life.* **Proverbs 4:13** *(emphasis added)*

Become a Mountain Conqueror

Instruction brings victory into a believer's life. Teaching waters God's divine seeds in the human heart and causes growth and strengthening. Jesus said:

If you abide in My word, you are My disciples indeed. And you shall know the truth, and the truth shall make you free.
John 8:31-32

Jesus said His disciples would be free. Free from what? I believe those who continue to be taught God's Word will gain knowledge of the truth and will become free from the bondages of the devil.

I love the story I heard once of a climber who tried numerous times to make it to the summit of Mount Everest. After each failure, he evaluated what he had learned and tried again. This man had many supporters who continued to back his expeditions.

Before leaving his homeland to climb Everest, the time he finally made it to the summit, he gathered his friends for

a special dinner. After the meal, he stood to address this
supportive audience. Behind him was a huge photo of Mount
Everest. During his speech, he turned around and spoke to that
picture of the world's highest mountain. These were his words:
"Mount Everest, I will conquer you, because you cannot get any
bigger but I can."

There is great spiritual truth in this story. All of us face huge
mountains in our lives. They can be mountains of doubt, fear,
sickness, depression, debt, failure, etc. Although we may not
be strong enough to overcome our mountains, through God's
Word, our faith and understanding can grow to the place where
we can conquer every enemy. Growth to a place of victory
through the teaching of God's Word is a key part of unlocking
the Abraham promise.

Being a Mountain Mover

While on the subject of mountains and the power and truth
of God's Word, I wanted to share with you a true story which
I had read when I was in seminary but had never been able to
get verification on until recently. I received a newsletter[5] from
a United Kingdom minister by the name of David Hathaway. I
will let him tell in his own words how he came across this same
story.

> *Thirty years ago I was put in a communist prison in*
> *Czechoslovakia. They said if I did not give up my faith, they*
> *would not let me out alive - the only way to get out was to*
> *become a communist! They gave me books to re-educate me,*

one of which was the true story of Marco Polo (a merchant venturer from Italy 1254-1354) and his travels in China with the Emperor, Kublai Khan, grandson of Genghis Khan.

One day the Chinese Emperor and Marco Polo came to a village and found a small group of believers. The Emperor was very cruel and commanded his soldiers to kill them. But, he said, "Before I kill you, I will prove that your God is dead and your Bible is a lie. Your Bible says, 'If you've got faith like a mustard seed, you will see a mountain and command it to move, and it will go.' Outside your village is a mountain - I'm going to give you three days to move it!"

The believers had three days to move the mountain! So Marco Polo said that they cried out the first day, "Oh, God, we're going to die, move the mountain!" And the mountain did not move. The second day, they found one man 'more spiritual' than the rest and they made him do the praying. He prayed all day, "Oh, God, we're going to die, move the mountain!" And still the mountain did not move.

The third day, the Emperor came back, commanded his soldiers to line the believers up outside the village and cut off their heads!

"But first," he said, "I gave you three days to move the mountain and it's still there! You have no God, your Bible is a lie, and I want you to die knowing that there is no God - you must pray one more time whilst I watch you! Then I'll kill you."

In that communist prison, with no Bible, this is what I read: Marco Polo said that this time those believers began to pray differently. They looked at that mountain, and began to command it to move in the name of Jesus! As the Emperor watched, the mountain MOVED! He became a believer and sent Marco Polo back to bring missionaries to evangelize China. Because of that one miracle, the whole nation was opened to the Gospel and today there are more than 100 million believers in China! Why? Because God moved the mountain!

This story so inspired David Hathaway's faith that he began to speak to the mountain enemy of his imprisonment. After only one year, the prime minister of England flew to Prague to secure his release. Hathaway flew back to the United Kingdom with the prime minister and ended up on television and in the newspapers declaring the miracle God had done.

This is a wonderful illustration of what will happen when God's Word takes root in a person. If they keep feeding their faith and listening to good teaching, that Word will grow until it is strong enough to move every mountain and bring victory over every opposition. In this manner, they will start to see the reality of possessing the gates of their enemies.

Chapter 7
Languages

If the power of God's Word is unlocked through teaching and understanding then we must look a little at a major obstacle to understanding and that is language. Language is the greatest barrier to understanding between people in our world today. This goes all the way back to the tower of Babel where God confused the languages of people in Genesis 11:9. Sadly, if a person does not understand your language, the truth you speak will have no meaning or relevance to them.

Many years ago, I was studying the first day of the New Testament church described in Acts chapter 2. I suddenly realized that apart from tongues of fire, there was only one great miracle on the day of Pentecost. It was not unknown tongues but rather *known* tongues.

The Bible describes the context of what happened on the day of Pentecost by saying there were, "***dwelling in Jerusalem Jews, devout men, from every nation under heaven." Acts 2:5*** *(emphasis added)*. If you were a devout Jew, and lived in Jerusalem, then you would almost definitely speak Hebrew or Aramaic. That means that many of those ministered to on the day of Pentecost spoke at least two languages – Hebrew or Aramaic and their mother tongue.

When Peter preached, everybody understood him because he spoke in Hebrew or Aramaic. However, the miracle that opened their hearts was that they had just heard the message in their mother tongue. Three times it is mentioned in Acts 2 that the people heard the message in their "**own language**" (Acts 2:6); their "**own language in which we were born**" (Acts 2:8); and in their "**own tongues**" (Acts 2:11) (emphasis added).

Of all the miracles God could have chosen to launch His New Testament church, he chose only one: putting the gospel into the languages of the people present. With Pentecost, I believe God gave us a HUGE key. In order to make the Gospel understandable in any nation, we must translate it into the birth languages of each people group. This is a critical step towards winning unbelievers and towards teaching believers.

Practical Tools to Reach and Teach Nations in Their Mother Tongue

Understanding any key in God's Word brings about a responsibility to use it. One practical result of this revelation about language in our ministry was that we created our ISOM video Bible school curriculum in a bilingual format. We used many well-known English-speaking teachers, and about twelve feet to their side we had a Spanish interpreter. The interpreter's voice could be removed in post-production and provided a translation time-gap. This format enables us now, with a good live interpreter, to insert into that gap any language on earth.

There are over 6,000 living languages in the world each spoken by more than 10,000 people. Those who have the truth of God's Word need to take responsibility to reach and teach those who have little or none of God's Word in their language. It would not be right to go any further in this section without

> *"... there was only one great miracle on the day of Pentecost. It was not unknown tongues but rather known tongues."*

mentioning the Wycliffe Bible translators and all the other frontline heroes who work so tirelessly to translate God's Word into foreign languages. I believe some of the biggest crowns in heaven will be handed out to these sacrificial warriors.

In the Introduction section of this book, I mentioned the *Jesus* movie produced by Campus Crusade for Christ. This film is probably the greatest evangelism tool ever developed for missionaries in our time. It is effective because people have troubled themselves to translate it into hundreds of languages. The result is that millions of people each year are being reached for Christ in their mother tongues. The efforts behind such tools need to be applauded and aided wherever possible.

Our ministry organization continues to work on another such evangelism tool called *God's Story*. This video was originally produced by Jeremiah Films but now operates under its own covering[6]. It is a narrative that uses a story-telling approach to give an overview of the Bible in about 80 minutes. Following what is known in missions circles as the chronological approach, this video does not just start with the life of Jesus. Rather it gives context to the sacrifice of Christ by first showing the fall of man in the Garden of Eden.

God's Story then uses well-known Old Testament stories to unfold the plan of salvation and the meaning of sacrifice. By the time the video shows the cross and the atoning work of Christ, the viewer already has been given an understanding of why Jesus had to suffer. Because this effective tool also was designed for foreign language translation, it too is having a great impact in many nations, especially those where people have never heard of Jesus before.

Christians must massively invest in bringing the salvation message and good teaching to the remotest parts of every nation in the mother languages of people. I encourage believers to utilize every translatable tool available to get the task of discipling the nations accomplished. I also encourage leaders to pour themselves and their resources into the development of materials that cross the language barriers and enable good teaching to be inexpensively made available to needy people. This is just one example of how understanding a key of the Abraham promise can help us develop practical tools to unlock it.

Chapter 8
Teaching in the Life of Christ

If the principle of teaching is so vital to unlocking the Abraham promise, then it should be found in the life of Christ. I did some research in this area and was amazed to discover the prolific nature of Christ's teaching ministry. Let's look at some Scriptures. To drive the point home, I have underlined the words daily, teach and teaching in each reference. These are just a few of many found in the gospels that reveal Christ's emphasis on teaching.

Now it came to pass, when Jesus finished commanding His twelve disciples, that He departed from there to teach and to preach in their cities. **Matthew: 11:1**

And Jesus, when He came out, saw a great multitude and was moved with compassion for them, because they were like sheep not having a shepherd. So He began to teach them many things. **Mark 6:34**

Then Jesus went about the cities and villages, teaching in their synagogues, preaching the Gospel of the Kingdom, and healing every sickness and every disease among the people. **Matthew 9:35**

And He marveled because of their unbelief. Then He went about the villages in a circuit, <u>teaching</u>. Mark 6:6

I was <u>daily</u> with you in the temple <u>teaching</u>, and you did not seize Me. But the Scriptures must be fulfilled. Mark 14:49

And He went through the cities and villages, <u>teaching</u>, and journeyed toward Jerusalem. Luke 13:22

And He was <u>teaching daily</u> in the temple. But the chief priests, the scribes, and the leaders of the people sought to destroy Him. Luke 19:47

And in the daytime He was teaching in the temple, but at night He went out and stayed on the mountain called Olivet. Luke 21:37

The teaching ministry of Jesus was hated and feared by the Jews. It ultimately drove them to have Him crucified. Luke 23:3 describes the moment when Jesus stood before Pilate after being accused by the Jews. Their initial accusation was that Christ was trying to make Himself a king. Since Rome recognized only Caesar as supreme king, they hoped their charge would be enough to have Him crucified.

> *"... The teaching ministry of Jesus was hated and feared by the Jews. It ultimately drove them to have Him crucified."*

Pilate knew the Jews did not care about the supremacy of Caesar. He knew there was a deeper reason for their malicious hatred of Jesus. In the following interchange, he masterfully revealed the real motive for the Jewish leaders' hatred of Christ.

Then Pilate asked Him, saying, "Are You the King of the Jews?" He (Jesus) answered him and said, "It is as you say." So Pilate said to the chief priests and the crowd, "I find no fault in this Man." But they were the more fierce, saying, "He stirs up the people, <u>teaching</u> throughout all Judea, beginning from Galilee to this place." **Luke 23:3**

Instead of reacting to Christ's answer that He was the king of the Jews, Pilate said he found no fault in Him. It was only then that the Jews showed their hand. It was the teaching ministry of Jesus that they hated and feared the most.

In His teaching Jesus revealed hypocrisy, imparted truth, and unveiled the real motives of the heart. Through teaching Christ brought revelation to ordinary people and disclosed the secrets of the kingdom. He revealed the true will of His Father and backed up His message with signs and wonders. His words brought hope, encouragement, warning, instruction, and life transformation. It is no wonder that during corrupt generations of church history, leaders have sought to silence the accurate teaching of God's Word and to remove its availability from all but an elite, corrupt few.

The Word of God does not bend for anyone. When Jesus taught, He set absolute standards and did not change them no matter how unpopular they were with the people. When I came across the following transcript, I was forced to reflect on this.

US Naval Communication[7]

This is the transcript of an ACTUAL radio conversation of a US naval ship with Canadian authorities off the coast of Newfoundland in October 1995.

Americans: Please divert your course 15 degrees to the North to avoid a collision.

Canadians: Recommend you divert YOUR course 15 degrees to the South to avoid a collision.

Americans: This is the Captain of a US Navy ship. I say again, divert YOUR course.

Canadians: No. I say again, you divert YOUR course.

Americans: This is the aircraft carrier USS Lincoln, the second largest ship in the United States Atlantic fleet. We are accompanied by three destroyers, three cruisers and numerous support vessels. I demand that you change your course 15 degrees north, that's one five degrees north, or counter-measures will be undertaken to ensure the safety of this ship.

Canadians: We are a lighthouse. Your call.

When the Word of God is our immovable lighthouse, when it is taught accurately, understood, and obeyed, personal blessings and God's promise of multiplication and victory will be released. There is, however, one final secret that needs to be understood when it comes to the watering and illumination of God's Word in our lives. It is the role of the Holy Spirit. Jesus made the following comment about Him.

But the Helper, the Holy Spirit, whom the Father will send in My name, He will teach *you all things, and bring to your remembrance all things that I said to you.* **John 14:26**

"... Through teaching Christ brought revelation to ordinary people and disclosed the secrets of the kingdom. He revealed the true will of His Father and backed up His message with signs and wonders. His words brought hope, encouragement, warning, instruction, and life transformation."

It is the Holy Spirit who brings the words of Jesus to life and teaches us what they really mean. In the example of Jesus expounding the Scriptures on the Emmaus road after the resurrection (Luke 24:32), the Holy Spirit is the One who caused the teachings of Jesus to burn inside the disciples. We will speak much more about the Holy Spirit in a later chapter. It just needs to be mentioned here that without His help, even great teachings will remain veiled and will lack power.

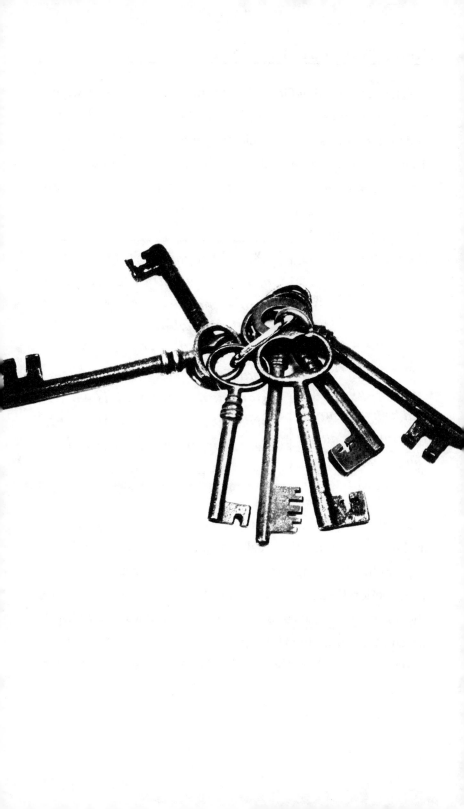

Chapter 9
Discipleship Multiplication

Key #2 – If Believers Make Disciples Who are Obedient, God Will Multiply Them

It is good to hear the truth of God's Word and be exposed to its content. It is even better to have a great teacher who can help you fully understand the Scriptures and what God expects in your behavior and attitudes. The next step is for your heart to fully believe and embrace the truth of what you understand. However, the ultimate goal is full obedience to the truth you have received.

When I was a child, my father built a safe room behind his study. It had a steel door about five inches thick. He kept all the family valuables there, including many beautiful pieces of jewelry, my father's wine collection, my grandfather's gun collection, and several heirlooms. My brother and I were seldom allowed to enter that room of treasures.

While away on a wilderness trip with a friend, my brother Graeme, who was about fifteen years old, stayed home alone. Now Graeme had a problem when it came to obeying rules. I can hardly remember a single week while going through high school together when he was not in some kind of trouble. That particular weekend, my brother found the key to the safe room and tried to unlock the 5-inch-thick steel door.

When the key wouldn't turn, Graeme got a pair of pliers and tried twisting the key with them. To his dismay, the pliers snapped off the head of the key while the body of the key remained in the lock. When my father found out what happened, his blood pressure rose to new heights.

Many Christians today hold the key to unlocking the Abraham promise but don't know how to unlock the door. They read God's Word, they are accurately taught the truths of Scripture, they understand God's requirements and believe all they are taught. Where they twist the head off the key is in the area of obedience to God's Word.

This principle goes back to the first five books of the Bible. Let's look at what Moses wrote in the Torah.

*Then it shall come to pass, because you listen to these judgments, and keep and do them, that the Lord your God will keep with you the covenant and the mercy which He swore to your fathers. And He will love you and bless you and **multiply** you.* **Deuteronomy 7:12-13** *(emphasis added)*

*Every commandment which I command you today you must be careful to observe, that you may live and **multiply**, and go in and possess the land of which the Lord swore to your fathers.* **Deuteronomy 8:1** *(emphasis added)*

Multiplication through Obedience

Obedience to God's Word and multiplication growth have always been closely linked. In fact, the original Abraham promise came through obedience.

*And in thy seed shall all the nations of the earth be blessed; because thou hast **obeyed** my voice.*
Genesis 22:18 (KJV) (emphasis added)

Some Christians want to relegate this principle to the Old Testament. However, the New Testament calls this concept discipleship. Discipleship is helping people to understand, believe, and most

> *"... Discipleship is helping people to understand, believe, and most importantly, obey God's ways."*

importantly, **obey** God's ways. This is the heart of the Great Commission, the final words Jesus spoke to His disciples.

*And Jesus came and spoke to them, saying, "All authority has been given to Me in heaven and on earth. Go therefore and make disciples of all the nations, baptizing them in the name of the Father and of the Son and of the Holy Spirit, **teaching them to observe all things that I have commanded you**; and lo, I am with you always, even to the end of the age."*
Matthew 28:18-20 (KJV) (emphasis added)

Jesus told His disciples to teach people what He had taught them. He also told them to be involved in teaching them *to observe* all the things He had commanded them.

The Greek word for "observe" is *Tereo*[8], which means "to attend to carefully." It is found seventy-five times in the New Testament. It is translated fifty-seven of those times as the English word *keep*. As you read the following verses from the books of John and Revelation, you will see how important it is for Christians to understand the true meaning of this word. I have bolded the word ***keep(s)*** in each verse for emphasis.

*Most assuredly, I say to you, if anyone **keeps** My word he shall never see death.* **John 8:51**

*If you love Me, **keep** My commandments.* **John 14:15**

*He who has My commandments and **keeps** them, it is he who loves Me. And he who loves Me will be loved by My Father, and I will love him and manifest Myself to him.* **John 14:21**

*Jesus answered and said to him, "If anyone loves Me, he will **keep** My word; and My Father will love him, and We will come to him and make Our home with him. He who does not love Me does not **keep** My words." **John 14:23-24***

*If you **keep** My commandments, you will abide in My love, just as I have kept My Father's commandments and abide in His love.* **John 15:10**

*Blessed is he who reads and those who hear the words of this prophecy, and **keep** those things which are written in it; for the time is near.* **Revelation 1:3**

*And he who overcomes, and **keeps** My works until the end, to him I will give power over the nations.* **Revelation 2:26**

Here is the patience of the saints; here are those who **keep** *the commandments of God and the faith of Jesus.* **Revelation 14:12**

*Behold, I am coming quickly! Blessed is he who **keeps** the words of the prophecy of this book.* **Revelation 22:7**

God's focus is not just on hearing, understanding, and believing, but on keeping the commandments of Christ. If we want to see the Abraham promise unlocked in our lives, we must fully obey Scripture. It is easy to blame individual believers for the rampant sin in today's church, but I think much of the blame falls on the shoulders of today's Christian leaders. In the Great Commission, Jesus gave the responsibility for discipling to His original eleven apostles. He said:

*Go therefore and **make** disciples of all the nations.* **Matthew 28:19** *(emphasis added)*

Jesus spent over three years pouring Himself into His disciples. He molded their lives and modeled His message before them. He knocked off many rough edges in their personalities, bringing them to a place of personal fruitfulness. Jesus prayed over the choosing of those people and took personal responsibility for their spiritual growth and welfare. When He died on the cross, Jesus left behind no worldly possessions, no real estate, no bank accounts, not even clothes. He left behind His words, the record of His deeds and eleven people He had discipled. At the

Great Commission, He charged those disciples with one major responsibility. He told them to **make** disciples.

We often expect that God will **make** disciples if we leave it up to Him. We figure each believer must take his or her own initiative. If they attend church, read God's Word, and pray, they will become disciples. Many church leaders today preach the Word of God and teach

> *"... When He died on the cross, Jesus left behind no worldly possessions, no real estate, no bank accounts, not even clothes. He left behind His words, the record of His deeds and eleven people He had discipled."*

its principles, but take little responsibility to help people observe and keep it.

A true discipleship process requires mentorship. It involves time, energy, and accountability. After praying all night, Jesus handpicked those into whom He was going to invest His time and energy. Mature Christians today, like Christ, need to seek those people whom God is calling them to disciple.

Now let's see the connection between the teaching of God's Word, the process of discipleship, and multiplication growth from the early church.

Then the word of God spread, and the number of the disciples ***multiplied greatly*** *in Jerusalem, and a great many of the priests were obedient to the faith.* ***Acts 6:7*** *(emphasis added)*

What a wonderfully rich Scripture! As God's Word waters the hearts of believers, and as they make the decision to keep the commandments of Christ, God does not just add disciples, He multiplies them. This principle is behind the massive growth of cell churches around the world. Cell or home group structures are essentially multiplication entities that facilitate the process of discipleship in the body of Christ.

As new Christians commit themselves to be accountable to more mature believers, true discipleship and mentorship can be facilitated. The result is a multiplication explosion. Some churches in Bogotá, Columbia, and in Seoul, Korea have grown to sizes in excess of 300,000 believers in a single congregation. God will multiply disciples if Christians commit themselves to **make** disciples.

Unlocking the Abraham Promise in Ephesus

Next to the life and example of Jesus, the greatest illustration of this discipleship principle comes from Paul's strategy in building the New Testament church at Ephesus. By analyzing the history of the Ephesian church, we can see why so many modern missionary efforts fail.

The story of Ephesus starts in Acts 18:18.

So Paul still remained a good while. Then he took leave of the brethren and sailed for Syria, and Priscilla and Aquila were with him. He had his hair cut off at Cenchrea, for he had taken a vow. And he came to Ephesus, and left them there; but he

himself entered the synagogue and reasoned with the Jews.
When they asked him to stay a longer time with them, he
did not consent, but took leave of them, saying, "I must by all
means keep this coming feast in Jerusalem; but I will return
again to you, God willing." And he sailed from Ephesus.
Acts 18:18-21

Many missionaries and international itinerant ministers
and evangelists today fly into a city for a few days and impart
a salvation seed or teaching. I praise God for any time that the
gospel is shared, but there needs to be more.

Paul, like most traveling ministers, had a busy schedule to
keep. His initial efforts resulted in a margin of response but little
long-lasting fruit. He did, however, leave Priscilla and Aquila
in Ephesus to follow up. Later our "watering" friend, Apollos,
arrived.

Now a certain Jew named Apollos, born at Alexandria, an
eloquent man and mighty in the Scriptures, came to Ephesus.
This man had been instructed in the way of the Lord; and being
fervent in spirit, he spoke and taught accurately the things
of the Lord, though he knew only the baptism of John. So he
began to speak boldly in the synagogue. When Aquila and
Priscilla heard him, they took him aside and explained to
him the way of God more accurately. And when he desired to
cross to Achaia, the brethren wrote, exhorting the disciples to
receive him; and when he arrived, he greatly helped those who
had believed through grace; for he vigorously refuted the Jews

publicly, showing from the Scriptures that Jesus is the Christ.
Acts 18:24-28

Apollos began watering the seed Paul had planted in the
hearts of the Ephesian believers. His knowledge of the Scriptures
was accurate but limited. It is encouraging to see that he was
open to correction from Aquila and Priscilla. But, like Paul, he
was an itinerant preacher and wanted to get back on the road.
He left before any significant growth could take place in the
hearts of the Ephesian believers.

Now things became really interesting in Ephesus when Paul
returned to this very strategic city (Acts 19). What follows is
probably the greatest revelation in the New Testament of the
Abraham multiplication promise being unlocked.

*And it came to pass, that, while Apollos was at Corinth, Paul
having passed through the upper coasts came to Ephesus: and
finding certain disciples, He said unto them, "Have ye received
the Holy Ghost since ye believed?" And they said unto him, "We
have not so much as heard whether there be any Holy Ghost."
And he said unto them, "Unto what then were ye baptized?"
And they said, "Unto John's baptism." Then said Paul, " John
verily baptized with the baptism of repentance, saying unto the
people, that they should believe on him which should come after
him, that is, on Christ Jesus." When they heard this, they were
baptized in the name of the Lord Jesus. And when Paul had laid
his hands upon them, the Holy Ghost came on them; and they
spake with tongues, and prophesied. And all the men were about
twelve. **Acts 19:1-7 (KJV)***

These twelve emaciated believers are the fruit of a visit from Paul, a visit from Apollos, and many months (possibly a few years) of labor by Aquila and Priscilla. At this point Paul began to utilize a divinely orchestrated strategy that eventually affected the entire region of Asia with the gospel message.

The School of Tyrannus

If the church today could learn from what Paul did in Ephesus, we would have the same results. Paul started by correcting their understanding of the Holy Spirit. The Ephesian believers had not received the promised baptism with the Holy Spirit (described in Acts 2). When Paul explained this gift to them and laid hands on them, they embraced this new truth and spoke with tongues and prophesied. Paul was then ready to engage the city of Ephesus with this small core of believers.

And he went into the synagogue and spoke boldly for three months, reasoning and persuading concerning the things of the kingdom of God. But when some were hardened and did not believe, but spoke evil of the Way before the multitude, he departed from them and withdrew the disciples, reasoning daily in the school of Tyrannus. And this continued for two years, so that all who dwelt in Asia heard the word of the Lord Jesus, both Jews and Greeks. **Acts 19:8-10** *(emphasis added)*

I wish Luke had added two chapters of explanation between verses nine and ten to tell us how this miraculous expansion across Asia happened. Paul preached to the large Jewish congregation in Ephesus for three months, then narrowed his focus to a small group he called disciples. He began teaching those believers daily in the school of Tyrannus. During a two-year period the Abraham promise was unlocked and a massive multiplication occurred. The whole of Asia was affected by this strategy.

Chapters like Acts 19 convince me that our two-year ISOM video Bible school is from God. This tool helps pastors train and equip disciples like Paul did in the school of Tyrannus. God supernaturally multiplied His Word to reach both Jews and Greeks across Asia. Today we are seeing God greatly multiply congregations in many parts of the world through a similar approach.

Let's now look at the progression of the discipleship program Paul conducted at the school of Tyrannus. Paul reasoned daily with the disciples. These believers were serious about the things of God. They were keen on learning God's Word, understanding it, and being obedient to what Paul taught.

There is not much written here about what Paul did, but let's look closely at what we do have in Acts 19:8. The King James Version of this verse gives us a good breakdown of the words used to describe this process.

And he went into the synagogue, and spoke boldly for the space of three months, disputing and persuading the things concerning the kingdom of God. Acts 19:8

The Greek word for "disputing" is *dialegomai*. It means "to ponder, revolve in your mind, converse, discourse, argue, and discuss[9]". These are the processes needed for disciples to understand what they are being taught. This process involves a two-way interaction with questions, answers, and discussions.

The second word used in this Acts 19:8 verse is "persuading." The Greek word is *peitho*, which means to "induce one by words to believe[10]". Paul wrote that faith comes by hearing

> "... *During a two-year period the Abraham promise was unlocked and a massive multiplication occurred. The whole of Asia was affected by this strategy.*"

and hearing by the Word of God (Romans 10:16). Paul was obviously involved in preaching and teaching in this school, as well as in discourse, interaction, and mentoring. As this seeding of God's Word happened with understanding into the hearts of believers in Ephesus, the revelation of truth expanded beyond the school of Tyrannus into the whole of Ephesus.

We do have one more glimpse into Paul's strategic methods in Ephesus and this is found in Acts 20. Paul's comments in that chapter go wider than the school of Tyrannus, encompassing the large Ephesian local church. Paul spoke the Acts 20 words during a subsequent missionary journey. He was passing close to the city of Ephesus, but did not have time to pay the church a visit. Instead, Paul called the elders of the Ephesian church to him. On a beach, he broke the news that he would never see their faces on earth again. Paul then reminded those leaders of key elements he had emphasized during his time with them. His farewell message is both moving and revealing.

And when they had come to him, he said to them: "You know, from the first day that I came to Asia, in what manner I always lived among you, serving the Lord with all humility, with many tears and trials which happened to me by the plotting of the Jews; how I kept back nothing that was helpful, but proclaimed it to you, and taught you publicly and from house to house, testifying to Jews, and also to Greeks, repentance toward God and faith toward our Lord Jesus Christ. Therefore I testify to you this day that I am innocent of the blood of all men. For I have not shunned to declare to you the whole counsel of God."
Acts 20:18-22

Paul described here the lifestyle of sacrifice he had displayed to the Ephesian believers. He re-iterated his emphasis on teaching the believers everything he knew. This was his method of helping them to stand as Christians in the midst of a hostile world. His teaching ministry was done both in public places, as well as in private homes. Through this example, we get a justification for cell or home groups, in addition to public services in a local church. The home meetings were places of instruction, and they facilitated personal ministry.

We also see from Acts 20 that Paul had trained and appointed elders to shepherd the flock. History tells us that Timothy was placed as the senior pastor of the Ephesian church. This shows the importance of having a good leadership structure when building a strong and influential local church. Paul had high standards for his leadership team. They are revealed in the qualifications he wrote to Timothy in 1 Timothy 3. Timothy got that letter while he was the lead pastor of the Ephesus church.

Paul also was very concerned that the Ephesian believers were taught true doctrine by godly people. He wanted those who taught to have right motives, and to be people walking in truth. He desired that all leaders would seek to build the kingdom of Christ and not their own kingdoms. Paul made it clear in the following verses that he continually warned the Ephesian Christians about the danger of false believers.

> *Paul was also very concerned that the Ephesian believers were taught true doctrine by godly people. He wanted those who taught to have right motives and to be people walking in truth.*

Therefore take heed to yourselves and to all the flock, among which the Holy Spirit has made you overseers, to shepherd the church of God which He purchased with His own blood. For I know this, that after my departure savage wolves will come in among you, not sparing the flock. Also from among yourselves men will rise up, speaking perverse things, to draw away the disciples after themselves. Therefore watch, and remember that for three years I did not cease to warn everyone night and day with tears. **Acts 20:26-31**

Events that Unlocked the Abraham Promise in Ephesus

The verses we just looked at contain keys to the huge influence of the Ephesian church in the first century. They also provide patterns for powerful, healthy churches today. Returning to Acts

19, let us look at the sequence of events that led to the unlocking
of the Abraham promise in that city. While Paul was teaching in
the school of Tyrannus, one of the first things that happened was
that God began something new in the life of the mentor/teacher
himself. Suddenly, the Holy Spirit added a fresh dimension of
power to the ministry of the apostle Paul.

*Now God worked unusual miracles by the hands of Paul, so that
even handkerchiefs or aprons were brought from his body to the
sick, and the diseases left them and the evil spirits went out of
them. Acts 19:11-12*

This is an interesting verse because, for most people, all
miracles are unusual. This Scripture points to the fact that God
has much more to offer Christians than they sometimes settle for.
He wants believers to experience new dimensions of His power.
These dimensions can be opened up in the lives of those who
commit themselves to accurately and sacrificially teach the Word
of God with right motives. It also can happen as believers grow,
through good teaching and discipleship, into maturity.

The Demonic World Shakes in Ephesus

Following this outpouring of the miraculous, the demonic
world began to be stirred up in the city. The message definitely
was expanding beyond the walls of the school of Tyrannus. The
anointing on Paul was so strong that, simply through contact
with a substance like a cloth, evil spirits fled from people and
healing was released into their bodies. We must assume that

people sent handkerchiefs because they were not able to get to where Paul was.

Paul's presence in Ephesus massively affected the spiritual powers in the city. Those dabbling in the occult were the next to confront the truth about Jesus that was multiplying in the region.

*Then some of the itinerant Jewish exorcists took it upon themselves to call the name of the Lord Jesus over those who had evil spirits, saying, "We exorcise you by the Jesus whom Paul preaches. "Also there were seven sons of Sceva, a Jewish chief priest, who did so. And the evil spirit answered and said, "Jesus I know, and Paul I know; but who are you?" Then the man in whom the evil spirit was leaped on them, overpowered them, and prevailed against them, so that they fled out of that house naked and wounded. **Acts 19:13-16**

Earlier in this book, we looked at what happened when Jehoshaphat started to passionately teach God's Word to the nation of Israel. After he sent leaders, chief fathers, Levites, and priests to teach, this was the result.

*And the fear of the Lord fell on all the kingdoms of the lands that were around Judah, so that they did not make war against Jehoshaphat. **2 Chronicles 17:10**

The same thing that happened with Jehoshaphat began to happen in Ephesus.

*This became known both to all Jews and Greeks dwelling in
Ephesus; and fear fell on them all, and the name of the Lord
Jesus was magnified.* **Acts 19:17**

As the knowledge of God's truth permeated the minds of
people in the city, a supernatural repentance gripped the region.

*And many who had believed came confessing and telling their
deeds. Also, many of those who had practiced magic brought
their books together and burned them in the sight of all. And
they counted up the value of them, and it totaled fifty thousand
pieces of silver.* **Acts 19:18-19**

When Bible truth reaches a certain point of penetration in
society, it starts changing people's thinking and habits. It brings
about repentance from occult practices and false beliefs. It is
only at this point that the Gospel starts accomplishing what it
was designed to do.

God's Word Prevails

We see in Ephesus how Paul's teaching began to dominate in
society, and God's Word became the norm in people's thinking
regarding right and wrong. What follows in Acts 19:20 is one of
the most awesome and significant verses in the entire Bible.

So the word of the Lord grew mightily and prevailed. **Acts 19:20**

The Word of the Lord has a life of its own. The more Paul
taught in the school of Tyrannus, the more the influence of the
school grew in the city. Disciples had the Word of God sown

into their hearts. They understood it, believed it, acted on it, and took it out into society. The result was an unlocking of the Abraham promise, an explosion of evangelism and discipleship. The impact was enormous, affecting a city, a region and all of Asia in a short period of about two years. This was not the end of the story, however. Let's see the next dimension of the Ephesus story in Acts 19 as God begins to shake the economy and the gods of the Ephesians through the preaching of the apostle Paul.

*And about that time there arose a great commotion about the Way. For a certain man named Demetrius, a silversmith, who made silver shrines of Diana, brought no small profit to the craftsmen. He called them together with the workers of similar occupations, and said: "Men, you know that we have our prosperity by this trade. Moreover you see and hear that **not only at Ephesus, but throughout almost all Asia, this Paul has persuaded and turned away many people, saying that they are not gods which are made with hands**. So not only is this trade of ours in danger of falling into disrepute, but also the temple of the great goddess Diana may be despised and her magnificence destroyed, whom all Asia and the world worship." Now when they heard this, they were full of wrath and cried out, saying, "Great is Diana of the Ephesians!" So the whole city was filled with confusion, and rushed into the theater with one accord. **Acts 19:23-29** (emphasis added)*

May we stir the gods of our society today through the preaching and teaching of God's Word and the discipleship of His people to a point where the pocketbooks of the industries

that support sin begin to cry out in pain. Wouldn't it be great
if abortion clinics, pornographic web sites, casinos, bars, and
drug dealers began going out of business because millions of
consumers repented and turned to God?

The church often has done things backwards. We go after
the sin-centers of our day, rather than focusing on the teaching
and discipleship of people. We must trust in the power of
God's Word. We
must believe
that when God's
Word is properly
sown and people
are discipled, the
miraculous will be
released, demonic
powers will be
shaken, repentance
will grip men's

> *May we stir the gods of our society
> today through the preaching and
> teaching of God's Word
> and the discipleship of His people
> to a point where the
> pocketbooks of the industries
> that support sin
> begin to cry out in pain.*

hearts, truth will prevail, and the demand for sin will diminish,
driving those who profit from it out of business. This unlocking
of the Abraham promise will cause a massive multiplication
of the Body of Christ, so that huge regions of the world will be
reached in short periods of time, just like in Ephesus. God has
sworn to do just that.

Chapter 10
Leadership Multiplication

Key #3 – God Will Multiply Leaders if the Church Prepares Leaders

Now we move beyond discipleship multiplication to leadership multiplication. Discipleship must come first. It is only through discipleship that the character of Christ develops in the heart of a believer. Many Christian leaders have fallen into scandalous sins because they became leaders before the character of Christ was formed in them. Jesus spent more than three years developing His image in His disciples before He commissioned them as leaders for the body of Christ.

When Moses chose leaders for Israel, he looked for people with three characteristics.

> *"... Many Christian leaders have fallen into scandalous sins because they became leaders before the character of Christ was formed in them."*

Moreover you shall select from all the people able men, such as fear God, men of truth, hating covetousness; and place such over them to be rulers of

*thousands, rulers of hundreds, rulers of fifties, and rulers of
tens.* **Exodus 18:21**

Jethro, Moses' father-in-law told Moses not to put anyone
into a position of leadership who was not known to be a person
of integrity and character. In the New Testament, twenty-eight
qualifications are given in the Pauline epistles with regards to
serving as a leader or elder in the body of Christ. Out of those
twenty-eight qualifications, eighteen are character qualities that
must be exhibited in the life of a believer.

God desires to multiply the impact of His people by making
their lives a leadership seed that He can sow. One of the most
significant parables in the New Testament dealing with the
seeding of leadership is that of the wheat and the tares.

*Another parable He put forth to them, saying: "The kingdom
of heaven is like a man who sowed good seed in his field; but
while men slept, his enemy came and sowed tares among the
wheat and went his way. But when the grain had sprouted and
produced a crop, then the tares also appeared. So the servants
of the owner came and said to him, 'Sir, did you not sow good
seed in your field? How then does it have tares?' He said to
them, 'An enemy has done this.' The servants said to him, ' Do
you want us then to go and gather them up? 'But he said, 'No,
lest while you gather up the tares you also uproot the wheat
with them. Let both grow together until the harvest, and at the
time of harvest I will say to the reapers, First gather together the
tares and bind them in bundles to burn them, but gather the
wheat into my barn."* **Matthew 13:24-30**

A few verses later, the disciples of Jesus asked about the meaning of this parable. Here is the explanation Jesus gave them.

*Then Jesus sent the multitude away and went into the house. And His disciples came to Him, saying, "Explain to us the parable of the tares of the field." He answered and said to them: "He who sows the good seed is the Son of Man. The field is the world, the good seeds are the sons of the kingdom, but the tares are the sons of the wicked one. The enemy who sowed them is the devil, the harvest is the end of the age, and the reapers are the angels. Therefore as the tares are gathered and burned in the fire, so it will be at the end of this age. The Son of Man will send out His angels, and they will gather out of His kingdom all things that offend, and those who practice lawlessness, and will cast them into the furnace of fire. There will be wailing and gnashing of teeth. Then the righteous will shine forth as the sun in the kingdom of their Father. He who has ears to hear, let him hear!" **Matthew 13:36-43**

Our tasks in God's kingdom have certain boundaries. There are some things we are supposed to do and other things only God can do. We are commanded to preach the gospel and sow the seed of God's Word. We cannot, however, force people to believe it or to obey it from their hearts.

When it comes to preparing leaders, we also have some boundaries. Our job is to prepare good seeds for Christ to sow. We are not to be sowers of people, only of God's Word. Sowing people is the job of Jesus, the Lord of the harvest.

Some denominations and missions agencies cross biblical
boundaries when they send people out without consulting
the Holy Spirit. They sometimes do not consider the heavenly
calling on the individual being sent. When this happens, man
usurps divine authority. The parable of the wheat and the tares
teaches that "He who sows the good seed is the **Son of Man**"
Matthew 13:37 (emphasis added). Jesus also told His disciples.

*The harvest truly is plentiful, but the laborers are few. Therefore
pray the **Lord of the harvest** to send out laborers into **His**
harvest. **Matthew 9:37-38** (emphasis added)*

When my wife and I were missionaries in Nigeria, some
pastors said all we needed to do was to pray for Jesus to send
laborers. "Where is Jesus supposed to get these laborers?"
I asked them. I told them they needed to go back to their
churches, choose at least twenty of their best members, and
spend the next two years sowing God's Word into those
believers. They needed to disciple, mentor, and train those
people for ministry.

I told them to bring those trained disciples to the front of the
church after two years, get on their knees and then pray, "Lord,
send **these** laborers, **these** good seeds I have prepared for You,
into Your harvest fields." Then they would see their trained
disciples suddenly receive callings from the Lord to the work
of the kingdom in other villages and regions of the country and
world.

This is where the unlocking of the Abraham promise comes in. If believers prepare good seeds for Christ, He will sow them. When Jesus sows a good seed into His field, the world, massive multiplication growth will happen. As Ken Kesey once said, "You can count the number of seeds in an apple, but you can't count the number of apples in a seed[11]."

Discovering the Hidden Treasures in God's People

"Treat people as if they were what they ought to be and you help them become what they are capable of being."

-Goethe-

It takes great skill and perception to prepare people to become good seeds. Jesus spent over three years preparing eleven good seeds before He gave them the Great Commission. In the gospel of Mark when Jesus called Andrew and Peter to be His disciples, He said, *Follow me and* **I will make you become** *fishers of men (Mark 1:17 emphasis added).* Jesus was confident that if they followed Him, He could mold their lives so they would become evangelists and reach people with the gospel message.

Just over three years later, on the day of Pentecost, Peter preached a message that swept over 3,000 souls into God's Kingdom (Acts 2). Jesus saw untapped leadership and gifting potential in Peter and Andrew and took responsibility to disciple that potential into fruition.

Believers need to prayerfully look into people's lives and see the deep deposits of God that lie waiting to be developed. People differ greatly in the way they see life, so no cookie-cutter approach can be used. The following amusing account illustrates this point of differing perspectives, but in the secular arena.

Technical Support[12]

A man is flying in a hot air balloon and realizes he is lost. He reduces his altitude and spots a man down below. He lowers the balloon farther and shouts, "Excuse me, can you tell me where I am?"

The man below says, "Yes, you're in a hot air balloon, hovering 30 feet above this field."

"You must work in Technical Support," says the balloonist.

"I do," replies the man. "How did you know?"

"Well," says the balloonist, "everything you have told me is technically correct, but completely useless."

The man below says, "You must be in management."

"I am," replies the balloonist. "How did you know?"

"Well", says the man, "you don't know where you are or where you're going, but you expect me to be able to help. You're still in the same position you were before we met, but now it's my fault."

Amusing, but it does illustrate the point. God has created everyone with different perspectives and potentials. The New Testament mentions five categories of leaders given by Christ to His church: These are commonly known as the five-fold ministry gifts. They are the apostle, the prophet, the evangelist, the pastor, and the teacher. These gifts are like gold mines hidden in the lives of God's people. It takes great wisdom by mature men and women of God to identify these treasures and to mine them to maturity. The Bible says the following about the function of these giftings.

And He (Jesus) Himself gave some to be apostles, some prophets, some evangelists, and some pastors and teachers, for the equipping of the saints for the work of ministry, for the edifying of the body of Christ, till we all come to the unity of the faith and of the knowledge of the Son of God, to a perfect man, to the measure of the stature of the fullness of Christ. **Ephesians 4:11-13**

> *"... Believers need to prayerfully look into people's lives and see the deep deposits of God that lie waiting to be developed."*

Equipping the Saints to Do the Work

Pastors are supposed to work with the other five-fold ministry positions to equip the saints and prepare seeds for Jesus to sow. Instead, many pastors have become the only real ministers in most churches.

I received a wonderful lesson about this when I was doing missions work in Nigeria. A church in Lagos started one of our video Bible schools with about forty students. Every Sunday, at the end of the morning service, the pastor had a special time of prayer for the sick. The line for prayer was always long. It sometimes took the pastor up to three hours to pray for all the needs of the people. Many times the person needing the most prayer at the end of the service was the exhausted pastor who was physically and spiritually spent.

That church began one of our video schools and after three weeks of training the pastor noticed that the students were learning how to pray for the sick. He suddenly had a great idea. He told the students they would be praying for the sick the following Sunday. The students were thrilled to have a chance to minister. Many of them fasted and prayed to prepare themselves. That Sunday, the pastor lined up the forty students at the front of the church and invited all the sick people in the service to come forward.

To his astonishment, over 40 miracle healings took place that Sunday, more than at any time he had prayed for the sick by himself. He then began to understand the Ephesians 4 Scripture about equipping the saints to do the work. For the first time in years, the pastor went home refreshed on a Sunday afternoon to enjoy time with his family.

God delights when we empower others to build His kingdom. In fact, some of the greatest miracles happen through ordinary saints who are correctly taught the Word of God. The church must become an equipped fighting force, knowing how to use spiritual weapons. This takes knowledge and training. No one would want an untrained doctor operating on them or an untrained pilot flying them. If we want people who are equipped in their professions in the secular world, how much more should we want

"... God delights when we empower others to build His kingdom."

trained people to minister to our spiritual needs. When people are properly prepared, Jesus has good seeds to sow, and great fruit is the result. In Nigeria we had some dramatic examples of ordinary believers who even while being trained, began to have a great impact in secular arenas.

In Enugu, Nigeria, a student in his first few months of our video Bible school training was on his way home in a crammed bus. Looking out the window he saw a madman standing naked in the bus station. The man, well known in the city as a demoniac, was carrying a sharp metal implement to intimidate people. The young student heard God's voice in his heart instructing him to cast out the demons in this man. He had just learned in class that if you obey the voice of the Holy Spirit, God will do the rest.

Before he had time to argue, he jumped off the bus and commanded the demons to depart from the demoniac. God's power hit that man and he was instantaneously delivered. Now in his right mind, the man crouched down, realizing he was naked. Those passing by who had witnessed this miracle were powerfully moved. Many of them reached into their pockets and took out money to give the man so he could buy some clothing.

A pastor's wife who lived in Lagos, Nigeria, used one of our video schools to train the leaders in their small church.

> "... The only way the harvest is going to be reaped is through a mass equipping of laborers of all ages."

To support her husband in the ministry, this lady had a job in a bank. But she kept complaining to the Lord about wanting to be in the ministry. One day God spoke to her about starting a ministry in the bank. She was puzzled, but eventually obeyed and began a lunchtime Bible study for bank employees. A few months later, she had won eight bank employees to Christ. When I ministered at their church, I personally led her Moslem bank manager to Jesus.

Any believer, young and old, can be equipped for ministry and developed as a leader. I know of twelve-year-old children who are preparing their lives for ministry and we have had saints in their eighties graduate from our schools. The only way the harvest is going to be reaped is through a mass equipping of laborers of all ages.

Leaders Should Confirm the Call of God

Not only is it a human function to prepare laborers and seeds for Jesus to sow, it is also a human function to confirm the call that God has given for people to go. In Acts 13 we see this dynamic principle clearly shown.

Now in the church that was at Antioch there were certain prophets and teachers: Barnabas, Simeon who was called Niger, Lucius of Cyrene, Manaen who had been brought up with Herod the tetrarch, and Saul. As they ministered to the Lord and fasted, the Holy Spirit said, "Now separate to Me Barnabas and Saul for the work to which I have called them." Then, having fasted and prayed, and laid hands on them, they sent them away. So, being sent out by the Holy Spirit, they went down to Seleucia, and from there they sailed to Cyprus. **Acts 13:1-4**

The Holy Spirit instructed the church leaders to lay hands on Paul and Barnabas and to confirm the call to go that God had given them. Wherever there is a true call, there should also be a witness to that call in the hearts of the church leadership. It

> *"... pastors need to be prepared to allow Jesus to send their most faithful people into the harvest. God will replenish these people if the pastor is unselfish with them."*

helps if the church leadership has an open ear to the Holy Spirit and a full understanding of the Biblical process. Many pastors and leaders have held on to people for selfish reasons, not releasing them into the harvest even when Jesus was sending them. This is the reason these early church leaders took time to fast and pray for confirmation.

There are times when a person is not ready for a call, or the candidate desiring the leadership's blessing is not biblically qualified. A good pastor or denominational leader can protect a person from being sent out prematurely or counsel a person to wait by not blessing their going. On the other hand, pastors need to be prepared to allow Jesus to send their most faithful people into the harvest. God will replenish these people if the pastor is unselfish with them.

A church I know in Alaska sent over 1,000 church members in teams to plant new churches. Every time they sent out good people, God replenished their ranks. When they stopped sending, God stopped replenishing.

A Bold Challenge for a New Approach to Leadership Development

Bill Hybels, pastor of one of America's largest churches, Willow Creek Community Church in Illinois, has rightly written, "The church is the hope of the world, and its renewal rests in the hands of its leaders[13]." Some of the methods Christians today are using to develop credible future leaders for the body of Christ will not get the job done. Fortunately, there are many groups that have made a transition to sensible leadership training strategies.

Leadership, or the lack of it, is the bottleneck of the global harvest and probably the greatest block right now to the unlocking of the Abraham promise in the body of Christ. Because many groups have wanted to preserve sound doctrine, they have followed institutional methods of leadership development. These often manifest themselves in either seminary or Bible school structures. Many of these institutions are divorced from the life of local churches and are addition, rather than multiplication, structures.

What many movements fail to understand is that a vast number of saints cannot leave their homes, jobs and families to attend a Bible school or seminary full time. Most of them have severe financial restraints, so only a small pool of young and inexperienced believers end up qualifying for ministry training.

In many nations of the world, hundreds of churches may belong to a single denomination or movement. If that denomination or movement is associated with a particular Bible School, all saints desiring to be recognized in that

> *"... God wants a mass equipping of laborers for the harvest, and we must change our old paradigms so God can multiply leaders."*

group will have to attend that school. I know one movement that has over 500 churches and about 200 students in their one two-year Bible school. By allowing only one way for leaders to get credentials, all that movement can do is add and not multiply their leadership base.

Let's take a hypothetical look at the 200 students in the Bible school I just mentioned. We will say about half are in their first year. Of the remaining 100, about 50 may be called to pastor. So in a good year, that school might graduate about 50 potential pastors. These graduates will hardly replace all the pastors of the movement's 500 churches who will retire, die or fail in one year. With this in mind, there may possibly be a net growth of ten new church plants or less. In order for the movement to grow, some pastors may have to pastor multiple congregations.

There is a better way! My counsel is to use media and technology to capture the best Bible school teachers of any movement on video, and to create extension programs in as many churches as possible. About 300 of the 500 churches could be turned into training centers, and each one can recruit at least twenty students. This would provide a pool of about 6,000 potential leaders. By using media, they can receive sound doctrinal training at a fraction of the cost of using live teachers. Pastors can then equip their saints at the local church level rather than sending them away to school.

In this way church leaders can unlock the Abraham promise and **multiply** leaders rather than just adding a few to the harvest. They could let their Bible schools focus on upper level training for equipping the generals and the lieutenants while the officers and soldiers are trained in the pews of local churches.

Pastors can be empowered if every possible church in a denomination or movement has the potential to become a ministry training center. Each church can equip their saints, and each pastor can develop the five-fold ministry gifts right in their own congregation. This is how any church can become a center for church planting and ministry sending, as the Lord of the harvest (Jesus) puts callings on the hearts of prepared seeds.

God wants a mass equipping of laborers for the harvest, and we must change our old paradigms so God can multiply leaders. Another problem that is solved when leaders are trained in the way I have described involves location. Often, when leaders leave rural towns to attend a training school in a major city or even abroad, they don't want to go back. When training is done in the villages, most students end up staying in their home environment and use what they have learned to reach and strengthen their own people.

What about Training the Two Billion Illiterate People?

The body of Christ has so gravitated to western models of instruction that they have largely cut out of the picture some two billion illiterate people in the nations. What is ironic is that many of those illiterate learners have richer faith, passion, and anointing than believers in our highest institutions of learning. It is time to bring the knowledge from the seminaries and Bible schools to the spiritually starving saints in remote places who have no access to God's Word. To do this, it may be necessary to make some radical changes and to modify some of the criteria for ministry recognition and ordination.

> *"... The body of Christ has so gravitated to western models of instruction that they have largely cut out of the picture some two billion illiterate people in the nations."*

On a practical level, this affected how we developed our ISOM material. Because it is video based, it can be used to train illiterate people. All our exams are in a multiple choice or true false format so they can be issued orally. We grant our diplomas to all students who qualify even if they don't read or write. We do want a sound understanding of the material but an experienced instructor can ascertain this. We encourage all Christian leaders to take on this challenge of making room for illiterate brothers and sisters to become equipped leaders in the body of Christ.

I want to conclude this section by again relating leadership development to the Abraham promise. When people become good seeds and are sown by the Lord of the harvest, Jesus Himself, into the world, a huge multiplication can begin to happen. These good seeds will begin to see the fulfillment of the promise Jesus made in the book of Mark.

So Jesus answered and said, "Assuredly, I say to you, there is no one who has left house or brothers or sisters or father or mother or wife or children or lands, for My sake and the Gospel's, who shall not receive a **hundredfold** *now in this time-houses and brothers and sisters and mothers and children and lands, with persecutions-and in the age to come, eternal life.* **Mark 10:29-30** *(emphasis added)*

The apostle Paul was sown by Christ into the Roman Empire and filled the known world of his day with the seeds of God's Word and young plantings of new believers and new churches in multiple cities and regions. He had homes wherever he went with his spiritual brothers and sisters and fathers and mothers.

It does not take much imagination to think of other plantings over the generations such as John Wesley, Martin Luther, David Livingston, Jonathan Edwards and even some modern day names such as Billy Graham, Reinhard Bonnke, Joyce Meyer, Bill Bright, Jack Hayford, Marilyn Hickey, T.L. Osborn, and Pat Robertson.

> *"... True good seeds planted by the Lord of the harvest into His field of the world have seen a massive multiplication growth of their ministries,"*

True good seeds planted by the Lord of the harvest into His field of the world have seen a massive multiplication growth of their ministries, some touching millions of souls. These people have truly unlocked the Abraham promise and blazed a trail for others to become similar seeds for Jesus to sow.

There is one major lesson that every fruitful seed sown by Christ into the world has had to discover. They have to die to themselves and conquer the sin nature in their personal lives. This death and resurrection process will be the subject of the next critical chapter.

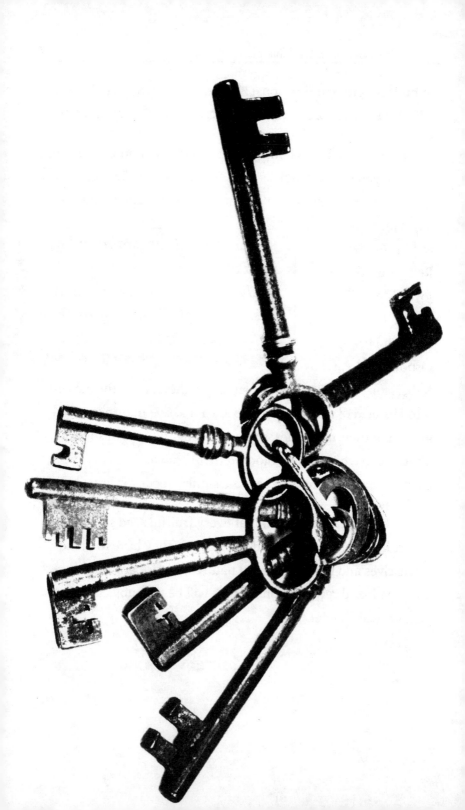

Chapter 11
Conquering the Sin Nature

Through the watering of teaching and discipleship, people begin to mature into the image of Christ in such a way that they develop into **good** seeds. Jesus is only looking for **good** seeds. In order for people to become these good seeds, they must undergo a painful process. They must die to their flesh nature. Jesus said the following.

*Most assuredly, I say to you, unless a grain of wheat falls into the ground and dies, it remains alone; but if it dies, it produces much grain. **John 12:24***

This putting to death of the flesh nature inherited from Adam is where many Christians struggle and few see real victory. This is also the reason the global church has such a dearth of good leaders who walk in victorious Christian living.

I struggled for many years with condemnation and a lack of victory over my flesh and over the seemingly uncontrollable thoughts of my mind. This was despite the fact that with all my heart I wanted to serve Christ and live in victory.

Most sincere Christians are caught where the apostle Paul found himself in Romans 7. Please note verses 17 and 20, which

I have bolded. They reveal perhaps the greatest secret I have learned to help a believer walk in victory over the flesh.

For we know that the law is spiritual, but I am carnal, sold under sin. For what I am doing, I do not understand. For what I will to do, that I do not practice; but what I hate, that I do. If, then, I do what I will not to do, I agree with the law that it is good. **But now, it is no longer I who do it, but sin that dwells in me.** *For I know that in me (that is, in my flesh) nothing good dwells; for to will is present with me, but how to perform what is good I do not find. For the good that I will to do, I do not do; but the evil I will not to do, that I practice. Now if I do what I will not to do,* **it is no longer I who do it, but sin that dwells in me.** *I find then a law, that evil is present with me, the one who wills to do good. For I delight in the law of God according to the inward man. But I see another law in my members, warring against the law of my mind, and bringing me into captivity to the law of sin which is in my members. O wretched man that I am! Who will deliver me from this body of death?* **Romans 7:14-24** *(emphasis added)*

In the following section, I have outlined four revelations that will help you put to death the flesh nature so that Christ's life can shine through you. These four revelations will set you free in your walk with Jesus Christ and will enable you to experience victory in your Christian life. These truths have revolutionized my walk with God and are the bedrock that has helped my ministry grow into an internationally impacting work.

Revelation #1 – Everyone has a sin nature inherited from Adam.

This may seem obvious, but it is critical for our understanding. Many Christians feel like everyone else has their life together, and only they are struggling. The truth is that even Billy Graham, Mother Theresa, and the Pope, have all inherited from Adam a sin nature, with all its ugly characteristics.

When I was a missionary serving in West Africa, I remember listening to a Nigerian man who had just escaped the civil war of Liberia. He described how he had been on a bus being held captive by terrorists. One of his captors decided to use the hostages for sport. He grabbed one man, thrust him off the bus, and told him to try to escape. As the man ran for his life, they shot him in the back like a hunted deer.

The terrorist who initiated this horrendous act then looked through the bus for another victim. God miraculously delivered this Nigerian man from the jaws of death, but when he told the riveting story to us, he made this simple statement. "When I looked into the eyes of that wicked terrorist, I saw what every human being has the potential to become without Christ."

"... When I looked into the eyes of that wicked terrorist, I saw what every human being has the potential to become without Christ."

Jeremiah wrote:

*"The heart is deceitful above all things, And desperately wicked;
Who can know it?" **Jeremiah 17:9***

When it comes to conquering that wicked and deceitful
nature of Adam, it is important to recognize that everyone has
it dwelling in them. There is no human being on the planet who
does not need to battle this enemy. God knows we all have this
sin nature; its existence does not take Him by surprise, and He is
on our side to overcome it.

Revelation #2 – Although the sin nature is in you, in God's eyes it is not you.

This is the most important revelation to grasp. Let's go back to
those verses from Romans chapter 7.

*If, then, I do what I will not to do, I agree with the law that it is
good. **But now, it is no longer I who do it, but sin that dwells
in me.** For I know that in me (that is, in my flesh) nothing good
dwells; for to will is present with me, but how to perform what
is good I do not find. For the good that I will to do, I do not do;
but the evil I will not to do, that I practice. Now if I do what I
will not to do, **it is no longer I who do it, but sin that dwells
in me.** Romans 7:16-20 (emphasis added)*

What is the apostle Paul saying? This is the heart of the
matter. He is saying that the sin nature is ***not him***. When a
person accepts Christ as Savior and Lord, that person becomes

a new creation in Christ. It is then that the sin nature, in God's eyes, is separated from the new believer and becomes dead to God because of the Cross.

God knows the sin nature was inherited from Adam and is full of wickedness and rebellion. What every Christian must understand is that God is on their side to defeat the influence of the sin nature in their life. God starts by no

> *"... The existence of the sin nature in a Christian is not sin in God's eyes, but yielding to the sin nature is sin in His eyes."*

longer considering that sin nature to be a part of the make up of a believer. The real person, from God's perspective, is that born-again new creation who wants to do right and wants to serve God.

Please pay close attention to the next statement. The **existence** of the sin nature in a Christian is **not** sin in God's eyes, but **yielding** to the sin nature **is** sin in His eyes. The **greatest lie** the devil will ever tell a Christian is that the existence of the sin nature is sin in God's eyes.

This is why many Christians are defeated. They want to be like God and follow Him. But whenever God's Word is preached, it illuminates sin in a person's life, reveals God's standard of conduct and exposes the wretchedness of the sin nature. Then the devil steps in with condemnation, telling Christians that God cannot possibly accept them due to all the sins they have. He convinces them that the sin nature in them **is them,** and

then wreaks havoc with their faith to the point that many doubt
their salvation. This brings me to the next revelation needed to
achieve victory over this vicious cycle.

Revelation #3 – You will never conquer the sin nature by force of will because you cannot overcome the flesh with the flesh.

Let me outline a scenario with which you may identify. A
believer is worshiping God in the sanctuary, doing his best to
focus on Jesus. A lustful thought comes to his mind, ruining
the intimacy of his worship. Condemnation follows, and the
believer tries to fight his thoughts and his imaginations. The
believer thinks, *If I can just get rid of these thoughts and put
them behind me, then I can get back to worshiping God*. He
throws Scriptures at the problem, tries to take authority over the
devil, and struggles to again experience God's glorious presence.
By this stage the worship moment has passed and the Christian
is left feeling defeated.

This struggle can easily escalate to where a believer is
continually fighting the sin nature. He or she is always struggling
because the devil tells the believer God can't accept anyone who
has such ungodly thoughts. He convinces Christians that the sin
nature in them *is them*.

Christians caught in this trap often run from God in shame.
They try to fix the problem with everything from positive
thinking to prayer and Bible reading. The harder they try to
control the thoughts and imaginations of the mind, the more

difficult it becomes and the more defeated in their Christian walk they become. Many believers either reach a stage where they wonder if they are still saved, or they resign themselves to a life without victory.

Why does God allow this cycle of defeat to happen? Because God will never allow a believer to conquer the sin nature by his or her own will and fleshly effort. If human effort could get the job done, man would take the credit for it. God makes it clear in Isaiah 42:8 that "I am the Lord: that is My name: and My glory will I not give to another."

In John 8:32, Jesus said, "You shall know the truth and the truth shall make you free." When we believe the lies of the devil, he can bring us into bondage. Only understanding and believing the truth will set us free. Paul told believers they needed to perceive themselves accurately, the way God saw them. He wrote:

Likewise you also, reckon yourselves to be dead indeed to sin, but alive to God in Christ Jesus our Lord. **Romans 6:11**

Paul is telling believers to think of their sin nature as being dead so they do not come under condemnation. This brings me to the fourth and final revelation that will bring victory.

Revelation #4 – The battle against the sin nature can only be won with the Holy Spirit's help.

When people are born again, God nails their sin to the cross and the old man dies. A new creation results which is the real person to whom heaven relates. The influence of the sin nature is still evident in the life of a believer but the new Christian now has a choice either to yield to the sin nature or to follow God's way as revealed in His Word, guided by His Spirit. Here is how Scripture paints this picture.

Sin is no longer your master, for you are no longer subject to the law, which enslaves you to sin. Instead, you are free by God's grace. So since God's grace has set us free from the law, does this mean we can go on sinning? Of course not! Don't you realize that whatever you choose to obey becomes your master? You can choose sin, which leads to death, or you can choose to obey God and receive his approval. Thank God! Once you were slaves of sin, but now you have obeyed with all your heart the new teaching God has given you. Now you are free from sin, your old master, and you have become slaves to your new master, righteousness. I speak this way, using the illustration of slaves and masters, because it is easy to understand. Before, you let yourselves be slaves of impurity and lawlessness. Now you must choose to be slaves of righteousness so that you will become holy.
Romans 6: 14-19 (NLT)

God's chief desire is to help believers understand how heaven views their sin nature. He wants to conquers its influence in a believer's life.

Let's return to our illustration of the brother in worship who has a lustful thought come through his mind. Instead of allowing condemnation to take hold of him, and starting the vicious cycle of fighting the flesh with the flesh, here is how he should deal with it. He should pray something like this: *"Lord, through these lustful thoughts, my sin nature is rearing its ugly head. Thank You that this sin nature is not me in Your eyes. I have no condemnation that its there. Thank You that You are on my side to defeat its influence in my life. I choose to yield to You, Holy Spirit, to deal with those thoughts. I know it is only through Your power that the flesh nature will be conquered in me. I put my trust in You now to see it happen."*

As believers learn to run to God for help in dealing with the sin nature and not away from Him, they will learn to do what the apostle Paul learned in Romans 8.

Therefore, brethren, we are debtors– not to the flesh, to live according to the flesh. **Romans 8:2**

*For if you live according to the flesh you will die; but if **by the Spirit** you put to death the deeds of the body, you will live. For as many as are led by the Spirit of God, these are sons of God.* **Romans 8:13-14** (emphasis added)

This process of yielding to the Holy Spirit's power and not coming under condemnation is easy in theory, but it takes time and effort to put it into practice. Paul begins Romans 8 with these words.

There is therefore now no condemnation to those who are
in Christ Jesus, who do not walk according to the flesh, but
according to the Spirit. For the law of the Spirit of life in Christ
Jesus has made me free from the law of sin and death.
Romans 8:1-2

God wants us to ask for His help in getting the sin nature
under control. When the Holy Spirit does it, God gets all the
glory. It is the third Person of the Trinity, and not ourselves, who puts to death the works of the flesh in us.

> *"... This process of yielding to the Holy Spirit's power and not coming under condemnation is easy in theory, but it takes time and effort to put it into practice."*

There has to be a death to the flesh nature in order for a
believer to become a fruitful seed. People must let God's Spirit
conquer their flesh nature so that God's nature can shine forth.
This death and resurrection process happens through these
revelations as well as through discipleship, trials, and learning to
live by faith and obedience to God's Word.

There is also another related area of study that may be helpful
to many believers and that has to do with iniquity. Many times,
when there is a specific propensity to sin in a family or an
individual, it is the result of iniquity that may have been passed
down from previous generations. Iniquity is different from
sin and transgression in the Bible. We are told to repent of
transgressions and sins but we are instructed to acknowledge

and confess our iniquity. God will forgive iniquity if we do this because Jesus bore our iniquities on the cross (Isaiah 53:11). I highly recommend a study book on this whole topic by A.L. and Joyce Gill called "Set Free From Iniquity" which is obtainable from Powerhouse Publishing[14].

As people die to their flesh nature and their own agendas, the divine life of God begins to dominate their hearts and lives. As this happens, they start becoming good seeds that Jesus can sow. This whole chapter, however, clearly shows how important the role of the Holy Spirit is in our lives. Without the Holy Spirit's help, a Christian is helpless and hopeless. This understanding sets the stage for us to look at the next major area that God wants to multiply. It is His anointing.

> *"... As people die to their flesh nature and their own agendas, the divine life of God begins to dominate their hearts and lives."*

Chapter 12
Anointing Multiplication

Key #4 – God Will Multiply Anointing if Believers Seek and Ask for It

Too many ministries today do not teach or talk about the anointing of the Holy Spirit. His function is critical to the release of the Abraham promise. The role of the Holy Spirit is so important that when Jesus ascended into heaven, He refused to let the disciples begin the work of the church without the following instructions.

Behold I send the Promise of my Father upon you; but tarry in the city of Jerusalem until you are endued with power from on high. **Luke 24:49**

The one main characteristic of the early church age was the outpouring of the Holy Spirit on all flesh. When the church was launched, the apostle Peter explained what was happening by quoting the Old Testament prophecy of Joel.

But this is what was spoken by the prophet Joel: "And it shall come to pass in the last days, says God, That I will pour out of My Spirit on all flesh; Your sons and your daughters shall prophesy, Your young men shall see visions, Your old men shall dream dreams. And on My menservants and on My maidservants I will pour out My Spirit in those days." Acts 2:16-18

Peter went on to say that this promise was for those who put their faith in Christ, even in subsequent generations.

For the promise is to you and to your children and to all who are afar off as many as the Lord our God will call. Acts 2:38

At the launch of the New Testament church, on the day of Pentecost, God released a multiplication of the Holy Spirit's anointing onto all people who would believe the simple gospel message and put their faith in Christ. There are different manifestations of the Holy Spirit's anointing and different ways to operate in those anointings. I define anointing as a divine grace deposit and enablement from the Holy Spirit.

Salvation Anointing

We will start at the point of salvation when every believer is given a deposit of the Holy Spirit. The Bible says Christians are born of the Spirit when they are born again.

For by one Spirit we were all baptized into one body– whether Jews or Greeks, whether slaves or free– and have all been made to drink into one Spirit. 1 Corinthians 12:13

At the point of accepting Jesus Christ as Savior and Lord, the Holy Spirit recreates a Christian's human spirit, and they become a part of Christ, a new creation in Him.

*Therefore, if anyone is in Christ, he is a **new** creation; old things*
*have passed away; behold, all things have become **new.***
2 Corinthians 5:17 *(emphasis added)*

So all Christian believers have the Holy Spirit anointing of
salvation in their lives.

Anointing Through Holy Spirit Baptism

The apostle Paul asked believers in Ephesus about this vital
experience.

And it came to pass, that, while Apollos was at Corinth, Paul
having passed through the upper coasts came to Ephesus: and
finding certain disciples, He said unto them, "Have ye received
*the Holy Ghost **since** ye believed?" And they said unto him, "We*
have not so much as heard whether there be any Holy Ghost.
"And he said unto them, "Unto what then were ye baptized?"
And they said, "Unto John's baptism." Then said Paul, " John
verily baptized with the baptism of repentance, saying unto the
people, that they should believe on him which should come after
him, that is, on Christ Jesus." When they heard this, they were
baptized in the name of the Lord Jesus. And when Paul had
laid his hands upon them, the Holy Ghost came on them; and
they spake with tongues, and prophesied. And all the men were
*about twelve. **Acts 19:1-7** (KJV)(emphasis added)*

When Paul came to the believers in Ephesus, he asked them
if they had received the Holy Spirit *since* they believed. This

clearly indicates that Paul considered receiving the Holy Spirit
an experience subsequent to their salvation.

When a person is saved, it is the Holy Spirit who baptizes
them into the body of Christ as described in the 1 Corinthians
Scripture we just looked at.

For by one Spirit we were all baptized into one body -
1 Corinthians 12:13

The gift of the baptism with Holy Spirit is received subsequent
to salvation and is similar to what was experienced by the
disciples on the day of Pentecost. After Jesus rose from the
dead, but before He ascended into heaven, He said this to His
disciples.

*"John truly baptized with water, but you shall be baptized with
the Holy Spirit not many days from now."* **Acts 1:5**

When Jesus made this statement, He was referring to the
baptism that He would personally administer to those who
believed in Him. When we look at the words of John the Baptist
concerning Jesus in the book of Matthew, we see a connection.

*"I indeed baptize you with water unto repentance, but He who
is coming after me is mightier than I, whose sandals I am not
worthy to carry. He will baptize you with the Holy Spirit and
fire."* **Matthew 3:11**

It is crucial to understand that at the point of salvation, it is
the Holy Spirit who baptizes a believer into Jesus. Subsequent to

salvation, it is Jesus who baptizes a believer into the Holy Spirit. These are two separate experiences.

The Bible describes a number of ways in which people received this anointing and immersion into the power of the Holy Spirit. The first way was through a sovereign work of God. That is what happened on the day of Pentecost as a fulfillment of that Feast. The people were praying, waiting for the promise of the Holy Spirit, and suddenly this wonderful gift was given from heaven.

I know people who have asked Jesus to baptize them with the Holy Spirit in the privacy of their own rooms and received on the spot the same gift Jesus gave at Pentecost. Jesus said,

*"If you then, being evil, know how to give good gifts to your children, how much more will your heavenly Father give the Holy Spirit to those who **ask** Him!"*
Luke 11:13 *(emphasis added)*

In Ephesus (Acts 19), when Paul laid his hands on the believers, they received the Holy Spirit baptism and spoke with new tongues and prophesied. This method of having a man or women of God pray and lay hands on you is another way a person can receive the anointing immersion from God and be baptized with the Holy Spirit.

A third way is described in Acts 11 when God gave this gift to the house of Cornelius. Peter was imparting knowledge of the message of Christ to his audience when this outpouring of God manifested.

*"And as I (Peter) began to speak, the Holy Spirit fell upon them,
as upon us at the beginning... Then I remembered the word of
the Lord, how He said, 'John indeed baptized with water, but
you shall be baptized with the Holy Spirit.' If therefore God gave
them the same gift as He gave us when we believed on the Lord
Jesus Christ, who was I that I could withstand God?"*
Acts 11:5, 16-17

So in summary, God multiplies His promise of the baptism
with the Holy Spirit in three major ways. The first is as a
sovereign act, the second is through the laying on of hands,
and the third as an impartation resulting from preaching and
teaching. Let's take a brief look at some other biblical examples of the multiplication of anointing.

> *"... at the point of salvation, it is
> the Holy Spirit who baptizes a
> believer into Jesus. Subsequent to
> salvation, it is Jesus who baptizes
> a believer into the Holy Spirit."*

Anointing for Leadership

When it came to leadership in the nation of Israel, there were
three major ways God anointed people. The first was by pouring
oil on an individual through the hands of a prophet. Anointing
oil has always been a type of the Holy Spirit. A clear illustration
of this is demonstrated when Samuel anointed both Saul and
David as king over Israel.

*Then Samuel took a flask of oil and poured it on his (Saul's)
head, and kissed him and said: "Is it not because the Lord has*

anointed you commander over His inheritance?"
1 Samuel 10:1

Then the Spirit of the Lord will come upon you, and you will prophesy with them and be turned into another man.
1 Samuel 10:6

Then Samuel took the horn of oil and anointed him in the midst of his brothers; and the Spirit of the Lord came upon **David** *from that day forward.* **1 Samuel 16:13**

The second way God imparted leadership anointing was through the laying on of hands. This happened when Moses transferred the leadership mantle to Joshua.

*Now Joshua the son of Nun was full of the spirit of wisdom, for Moses had laid his **hands** on him; so the children of Israel heeded him, and did as the Lord had commanded Moses.*
Deuteronomy 34:9

The third way God imparted anointing for leadership is especially relevant to us today. It unlocks a secret that is greatly needed in the body of Christ.

When Moses had brought the children of Israel out of Egypt, he tried to manage the nation almost single handedly. Fortunately, he had a wise father-in-law named Jethro who gave him some great administrative advice. The following passage explains what Moses did in response to the advice of Jethro.

And Moses chose able men out of all Israel, and made them heads over the people: rulers of thousands, rulers of hundreds, rulers of fifties, and rulers of tens. So they judged the people at all times; the hard cases they brought to Moses, but they judged every small case themselves. **Exodus 18:25-26**

Moses developed an administrative system to govern the nation of Israel. But he did not ask for a multiplication of his leadership anointing. So, although he had leaders in appointed positions, he was at his wits end just a short time later.

So Moses said to the Lord, "Why have You afflicted Your servant? And why have I not found favor in Your sight, that You have laid the burden of all these people on me? Did I conceive all these people? Did I beget them, that You should say to me, 'Carry them in your bosom, as a guardian carries a nursing child,' to the land which You swore to their fathers? Where am I to get meat to give to all these people? For they weep all over me, saying, 'Give us meat, that we may eat.' I am not able to bear all these people alone, because the burden is too heavy for me. If You treat me like this, please kill me here and now— if I have found favor in Your sight— and do not let me see my wretchedness!" **Numbers 11:11-15**

Many Christian leaders today have good administrative structures, but still carry the load. They have not prayed for God to multiply their anointing to lead into those under them. Others may have made poor administrative choices resulting in an abnormally influential board of deacons. Look at the solution God gives Moses.

So the Lord said to Moses: "Gather to Me seventy men of the elders of Israel, whom you know to be the elders of the people and officers over them; bring them to the tabernacle of meeting, that they may stand there with you. Then I will come down and talk with you there. I will take of the Spirit that is upon you and will put the same upon them; and they shall bear the burden of the people with you, that you may not bear it yourself alone..."
Numbers 11:16-17

So Moses went out and told the people the words of the Lord, and he gathered the seventy men of the elders of the people and placed them around the tabernacle. Then the Lord came down in the cloud, and spoke to him, and took of the Spirit that was upon him, and placed the same upon the seventy elders; and it happened, when the Spirit rested upon them, that they prophesied...
Numbers 11:24-25

> *"... God provided a 7,000 percent multiplication of the anointing of Moses. The Bible does not say that each person received one seventieth of his anointing, they each got the same Spirit that was on Moses."*

God provided a 7,000 percent multiplication of the anointing of Moses. The Bible does not say that each person received one seventieth of his anointing, they each got the **same** Spirit that was on Moses.

God did not choose who would receive this impartation of anointing. In Numbers 11:16, God told Moses to choose and gather the seventy people based on his knowledge of their

character and leadership positions. Christian leaders today
need to follow this pattern and choose people into whom God
can multiply their anointing. That anointing multiplication can
happen through the laying on of hands, through prayer, and
through asking God to share across many shoulders the burdens
of leadership by multiplying the anointing needed to carry those
burdens.

Anointing for Different Types of Ministry

Jesus was the supremely anointed One. In fact the word *Christ*
means "anointed." When Jesus started His earthly ministry,
He quoted a verse from the book of Isaiah. Through it He
revealed some of the areas of ministry He had been anointed to
accomplish.

*"The Spirit of the Lord is upon Me, Because He has anointed
Me to preach the Gospel to the poor; He has sent Me to heal the
brokenhearted, to proclaim liberty to the captives and recovery
of sight to the blind, to set at liberty those who are oppressed; To
proclaim the acceptable year of the Lord." **Luke 4:18-19***

Different ministries in the body of Christ carry different
types of anointing. For example, when a person greatly used in
worship imparts teaching in his or her area of expertise, there
is a tangible manifestation of a worship anointing in the room
where the teaching is conducted. This principle even works
when using video. There is a multiplication of the anointing
of the teacher into the students as they sit under teaching in
a specific area of training. That anointing may be for prayer,

healing, worship, leadership, evangelism, miracle healing, or for some another area of ministry.

In our video Bible school, we chose anointed teachers in many different areas of ministry so there would be a multiplication of those anointings into believers all over the world. Many times in the live recordings we had the instructors lay hands on the people present. We also had them pray to the cameras to impart an anointing to the video students. After many testimonies, we discovered that God multiplies His anointing even through the video medium.

Paul wrote about this principle of anointing multiplication in the book of Romans.

*For I long to see you, that I may **impart** to you some spiritual gift, so that you may be established.*
***Romans 1:11** (emphasis added)*

Paul knew God would impart the gifts of the Holy Spirit through him. He carried an anointing from God, and he greatly desired to see what he had been graced by God with multiplied into the lives of others. Paul also wrote to Timothy:

*Therefore I remind you to stir up the gift of God which is in you through the laying on of my hands. **2 Timothy 1:6***

Again, he wrote:

Do not neglect the gift that is in you, which was given to you by prophecy with the laying on of the hands of the eldership.
1 Timothy 4:14

Here we see anointing multiplication through the hands of
Paul and through the hands of the eldership. Church leaders
today need to pray for God to multiply their anointings into the
lives of faithful people.

Often leaders do not fully realize the power of what they are
imparting through their prayers. In Acts 6, the apostles needed
people who would administrate the church so they could give
themselves to prayer and the ministry of the Word. They chose
seven men and laid hands on them. Two of those men were Stephen and Phillip. Let's look at the scriptural description of this scene.

> *"... we see in Scripture that people can put a demand on the anointing. Elisha asked for a double portion of the anointing that was on Elijah, and he received it"*

*Then the twelve summoned the multitude of the disciples and
said, "It is not desirable that we should leave the Word of God
and serve tables. Therefore, brethren, seek out from among
you seven men of good reputation, full of the Holy Spirit and
wisdom, whom we may appoint over this business; but we will
give ourselves continually to prayer and to the ministry of the
Word." And the saying pleased the whole multitude. And they
chose Stephen, a man full of faith and the Holy Spirit, and
Philip, Prochorus, Nicanor, Timon, Parmenas, and Nicolas, a
proselyte from Antioch, whom they set before the apostles; and
when they had prayed, they laid hands on them. Acts 6:2-6*

The apostles told the multitude to seek out people of good character to be candidates for anointing impartation. There was, however, a clear process involved. First the apostles defined the problem. They then laid out the requirements for the positions they were seeking. At this point they had the congregation nominate seven candidates, which the apostles subsequently confirmed by laying hands on them. Again it is important to note that it was the people and not God who chose these leaders based on their reputations. A few verses later; we see that God gave one of the seven, Stephen, more than just a token blessing when hands were laid on him.

And Stephen, full of faith and power, did great wonders and signs among the people. **Acts 6:8**

Phillip also moved into a new dimension of ministry.

Then Philip went down to the city of Samaria and preached Christ to them. And the multitudes with one accord heeded the things spoken by Philip, hearing and seeing the miracles which he did. For unclean spirits, crying with a loud voice, came out of many who were possessed; and many who were paralyzed and lame were healed. And there was great joy in that city. **Acts 8:5-8**

Finally, we see in Scripture that people can put a demand on the anointing. Elisha asked for a double portion of the anointing that was on Elijah, and he received it (2 Kings 2:9). The woman with the issue of blood, by faith, put a demand on the healing anointing that was in Jesus. Even though hundreds of people were touching Him in the crowd, the moment she touched Jesus, God's anointing flowed into her body and healed her (Luke 8:43 and Matthew 9:20).

A person who desires the anointing can ask others with anointing to pray for them and lay hands on them. They can also, by faith, put a demand on the anointing in the lives of others and receive a multiplication of that anointing into their own lives without anyone touching them. However, people can lose the anointing if they do not keep their character in check. Samson was greatly anointed but his wayward lifestyle and perverted relationships finally undid him and the Holy Spirit's anointing of supernatural strength departed from him.

We may not fully understand the anointing of the Holy Spirit, but we do know that it does make a difference. Bible scholars have pointed out that twice the number of miracles are recorded about Elisha than about Elijah. This is very likely due to the double portion of anointing he received.

Even though David was anointed as a young shepherd boy, the anointing of God made a difference in his life. It was reflected in his music, his writing, his ruling and his ability to fight his enemies. He still had to go through the character molding of discipleship, but the anointing added a huge dimension to who he became.

Today's believers need to seek the anointing of God, ask for it, and believe God for a multiplication impartation from other anointed saints into their own lives. Once we have an anointing from God, we should seek to have our anointing multiplied into the lives of other godly, hungry believers. God will multiply His anointing because the Father desires to see His Holy Spirit poured out on **all** flesh.

Chapter 13
Church Multiplication

Key #5 – God Will Multiply Churches if Believers Plant New Churches

*Then the churches throughout all Judea, Galilee, and Samaria had peace and were edified. And walking in the fear of the Lord and in the comfort of the Holy Spirit, they were **multiplied**. Acts 9:31 (emphasis added)*

One lesson missiologists have learned over the past fifty years is the power of church planting. The world-renowned church growth expert, Dr. C. Peter Wagner has repeatedly said.

> *"The most effective evangelistic methodology under heaven is to plant new churches[15]."*

Church planting was certainly the strategy of the early church. We have covered in this book the sowing of the Word of God, the making of disciples, the development of leaders and the anointing of those leaders. The purpose of this process is to enable Jesus to sow leaders into the harvest so new churches and ministries can be birthed. Prayerfully this process will be repeated again and again.

I believe passionately in the local church. I am not referring to buildings where people attend church services. The church is the gathering of Christian believers anywhere in the world for the purpose of encouraging one another, worshipping, fellowshipping, praying together, and feeding people God's life-giving Word. A church may meet in a building, in a basement, or under a tree. The venue is not so important as the function of believers gathering together around the lordship of Christ and conducting their gatherings according to a pattern consistent with what is taught in the New Testament.

The local church is the building block of the worldwide body of Christ. When Jesus spoke to the global church in the book of Revelation, he did so through seven local churches. The establishment of strong neighborhood churches in every community around the world is currently one of the highest goals of world missions.

My Journey to Discover Church Planting as a Strategy

I became convinced about the strategy of church planting after working for over three years as the television producer for German evangelist Reinhard Bonnke. He conducts mass evangelism crusades in Africa and has had crowds as large as 1.6 million

> *"... The local church is the building block of the worldwide body of Christ. When Jesus spoke to the global church in the book of Revelation, he did so through seven local churches."*

people in a single service. During my years with Reinhard, I saw millions come to a genuine new faith in Christ. Bonnke was doing his part of the harvest work as an evangelist, but my heart cried out for the millions of newborn sheep who needed shepherds.

As I prayed about what to do, I recognized there were pieces of the harvest puzzle that were missing in my understanding. The desire to know how to more effectively disciple people caused me to leave my work in Germany and take my family to Pasadena, California, for two years of study at Fuller Theological Seminary. That happened in the early 1990s when Dr. C. Peter Wagner and many other great missiologists were at Fuller. Before long I was up to my eyeballs in church-growth and church-planting literature and classes.

While attending Fuller, an opportunity presented itself for me to travel to the Philippines. My task was to document the history of the DAWN 2000 movement. DAWN stands for Discipling a Whole Nation. The founder, Jim Montgomery, helped mobilize the churches in the Philippines to plant 50,000 new churches in that nation between 1976 and the year 2000.

Before leaving for the Philippines to film the documentary, I had the honor of interviewing Dr. Donald McGavran, considered by many to be the father of the modern church-growth movement. He wrote the classic book *Bridges of God*, about how to penetrate into unreached people groups. He was ninety-two years old when I went to record a television interview with him. It was his last interview. Two weeks later he went home to be with the Lord.

Dr. McGavran was an incredible man of God. In the interview, he beat the same drum that had made him a living legend. He talked about the Great Commission and the need to disciple every people group on the planet. He pointed out that the word nations in the Great Commission's mandate to "make disciples of all nations," refers to people groups or tribes, not just countries. He stressed the need to establish local churches among every people group and in every geographic locale on earth. He said these churches needed to fit the culture and context of the people being reached.

> *"... The word nations in the Great Commission's mandate to, "make disciples of all nations," refers to people groups or tribes, not just countries."*

The multiplication of local churches is a cry of the DAWN 2000 movement and it subsequently became a pillar of the "AD2000 and Beyond" movement led by Dr. Louis Bush. DAWN's founder, Jim Montgomery, utilized the Barangay neighborhood political structure of the Philippines as the basis for his vision. He challenged the national leadership of the church to plant a Bible-believing church in every Barangay. The churches in the Philippines rallied around the vision and goal. In about twenty-four years, they planted over 50,000 new churches in the country.

Despite the great power and impact of the DAWN vision, there was one problem with the strategy. DAWN provided very little help when it came to leadership development, expecting each local church or denomination to solve this problem for themselves. After the turn of the millennium, one of our ministry representatives for the Philippines, J.C. Sterley, attended a DAWN Congress in that nation. The gathering was brought together to celebrate and evaluate the fruit of the DAWN strategy. Here is a copy of the e-mail I received from him:

Dear Pastor Berin,

At the Dawn Congress the message that sounded LOUD and CLEAR was that, yes, we did achieve the goals of planting more than 50,000 churches from 1976 to 2000, but 28,000 have not got Bible school graduates leading them, and the overall health of the local church is not very good. Of the 13,000 plus churches planted in the '80s, 6,000 no longer exist. So the focus for the next stretch is developing healthy churches to reproduce healthy churches.

A Practical Church Planting Model

Through the DAWN documentary experience, and all the facts and research I studied at Fuller, I became convinced that church planting was the most fruitful and effective evangelistic strategy under heaven. What was missing in my understanding was how to get the job done.

Then I read a book at Fuller that changed my life. *The Team Method of Church Planting*[17] was a doctoral thesis done by Dr. Jim Feeney telling how their church in Anchorage, Alaska, had sent out over 1,000 members in teams to plant new churches. Their basic model consisted of two simple steps:

1) Turn the local church into a ministry training center.

2) Turn the local church into a church-planting center.

When a local church becomes a ministry training center, it has a destiny. That destiny is the preparation of seeds through discipleship and five-fold ministry input. The purpose of seed preparation is so that Jesus can send those seeds out in teams to plant new churches.

Discovering this model changed my thinking. What if every church on the planet could send at least some of their members to establish other churches. Then we would start seeing a multiplication of churches.

This is why I designed the ISOM curriculum as a tool to help turn every church into a world-class ministry training center. By adding a course to the curriculum by Dr. Jim Feeney on "The Team Method of Church Planting," I put software inside the ISOM program to help each congregation move to step two: turning the church into a church-planting center. This two-step process continues to be our focus around the globe.

God will multiply churches if people commit themselves to planting churches. It will not happen spontaneously. Church leaders must make church planting a priority and view it as a critical part of what God has commanded them to do.

All Keys Must be Used Together

Church multiplication should be a natural byproduct of using the first four multiplication keys of the Abraham promise. As we saw in the Philippines, we cannot plant churches if we have not properly discipled people and prepared leaders. Any good church-based training curriculum will enable a church to use those first four keys. When they are properly used, the fifth key becomes feasible.

Many ministries focus primarily on key #1, the sowing of the Word. Because they do not put effort into accountable discipleship, they lose much of their fruit. A high percentage of new converts at mass evangelism crusades do not continue in their new faith and are not serving God in local churches five years later[16]. I support crusades, but they are only part of the picture. There will always be some multiplication when God's Word is sown, but never a full measure unless the other keys are used.

Some ministries focus on key #2, the discipleship of people, but do not plant churches. They end up with massive single churches with

> *"... if every church on the planet could send at least some of their members to establish other churches. Then we would start seeing a multiplication of churches."*

very little five-fold leadership development. Sadly, few people are sent out to plant healthy churches in needy parts of the world. Those churches see huge discipleship multiplication but limited church multiplication. They are fruitful, but they could become much more fruitful if they utilize the other keys.

Other groups focus on key #3, the development of leadership. Bible schools and seminaries sometimes fall into this category. When people entering such institutions have been well discipled, great fruit comes from their leadership training. Where poor discipleship has happened, students get a head full of knowledge, but their lack of character can ruin them.

Leadership development should always be built on the back of character development. We designed our video Bible schools to function in the local church, under the covering of a local pastor, because we did not want to divorce leadership development from the life of the local body. We understand that good pastors know their flock. They know if their sheep are faithful givers, whether their families are in order, and whether their reputations are above reproach. They are involved in the discipleship process and should therefore be in a good position to develop the leadership potential in their people.

Similar criticisms hold true for churches that focus too much on key #4, the multiplication of anointing. I am all for anointing multiplication, but in some churches people are falling over in manifestations of God's power, but they have little balanced teaching of the Word and hardly any real discipleship taking place.

People sometimes forget that although the anointing breaks the yoke of bondage over a person, it is truth that sets them free. God's power can deliver people from the influence of demonic spirits, but unless people understand their authority in Christ and repent of the behavior that opened the door to that influence, they will be in danger of falling back under that spiritual control. That is why knowledge and truth are so vital.

Many anointed ministers have ended up in sin because they were not properly discipled and never fully dealt with areas

> *"... The gifts and anointing of God will grow any church, but only leadership with character will keep a church over the long haul."*

of bondage in their lives. The gifts and anointing of God will grow any church, but only leadership with character will keep a church over the long haul.

Churches today need a balanced use of these powerful keys. If a church will do its part in all areas, the Abraham promise will be fully unlocked to them, and they will touch the nations of the world with massive multiplication impact. It is critical for local churches to recognize their strengths and to draw on other ministries to offset their weaknesses.

This is where parachurch ministries have a vital role to play. They can bring in mature anointings or five-fold emphases into a local church body. These parachurch ministries need to serve local churches with their gifts and understandings. Only as the

body of Christ draws on each vital part that God has placed in
the global church will it be balanced and healthy in its growth.

We Must Make Room for Apostolic Leadership

One final note on the multiplication of churches involves
the role of apostolic ministry. I have heard the comment that
the *Acts of the Apostles* was written because the apostles acted.
The early church was spearheaded by mature apostles and this
was a key to their success. They had an agenda to evangelize
and establish local churches wherever they went and the Bible
clearly reveals that apostles are especially graced for this task.

The body of Christ needs to again make room for apostolic
leadership that is able to spearhead and facilitate church
planting efforts. I am not talking about a top down authoritarian
approach taken today by some who call themselves apostles.
Rather we need spiritual fathers and mothers who love and
serve people. We need apostolic people who are willing to
sacrifice themselves, like the apostle Paul did, for the sake of
the gospel. Most of all we need those who have the goal of
developing and releasing the potential of others without legal
and money strings attached.

Chapter 14
Finances and Resource Multiplication

Key #6 – God Will Multiply Finances and Resources if Believers Sow Them into the Harvest

When my wife and I were serving God in Nigeria, we had dinner one evening with another missionary. To protect her identity I will call her Angela. At that time she was in her early forties. She had grown up in a rural area of the United States as one of four children. Angela's father had worked hard enough, but gave their mom only a measly allowance to feed and clothe the children.

Because of the father's miserly disposition toward money, the family lived on basic stipends like potatoes and rice. They seldom went out to dinner, and entertainment was almost non-existent. They never went on vacation, and the girls were allowed only one new outfit each year. Angela told us that her mother always desperately wanted to have a vacation in Hawaii, but the father refused to spend the money. Even when an aunt offered to pay for herself and take just her mother, the father refused to pay. Time passed, the children grew up and left home. Sadly, the mother developed cancer and died.

Angela went her way and eventually ended up doing missions work in Africa. When she was in her late thirties, she returned to the USA on furlough. While there, she received a call from her father who was a lonely old man living in Oregon. In the midst of her conversation, he asked her to lend him $10,000. After telling him she was a poor missionary with meager funds, she asked why he needed the money.

"If I could get my hands on just $10,000 more," he said, "I'll reach my goal of saving one million dollars."

Angela broke down and cried. All those years the family had lived in poverty, there had been plenty of money, but the father had a perverted obsession to hoard those funds rather than investing them in the lives of his family. His greed had resulted in misery.

Even though we were relatively poor missionaries ourselves at the time we heard this story, my wife and I changed our philosophy about money and resources. We decided we were going to seize every possible moment with our family to invest in their well-being, to travel and to enjoy opportunities when they came our way. We decided to take full advantage of each day of health and fellowship that God allowed us to have.

Wise Investments from Matthew 25

Matthew 25 contains three parables that all end in judgment. The first parable is that of the ten virgins. Five were wise and five were foolish. Because they were virgins, I must conclude that all were saved, but only five invested in preparing themselves for the return of their Master. It is clear from the parable that it cost money, time and effort for the wise virgins to get the oil. They could not obtain it by simply borrowing from one another.

I believe, like most scholars, that the oil in this parable refers to the anointing oil of God's Holy Spirit. One of the reasons I am so strong on Bible school training is because of this parable. I believe through studying God's Word under anointed instructors, together with mentoring and discipleship, that believers can start to carry the anointing of God in their lives.

> *"... It is clear from the parable that it cost money, time and effort for the wise virgins to get the oil. They could not obtain it by simply borrowing from one another."*

God is removing excuses from His people when it comes to ministry training. One of the goals of our ministry is to make training available and affordable to every believer on the planet. We are only one group out of many who are concentrating on offering cost effective options to Christians in this arena. The bottom line is that believers need to invest money, time, and resources into ministry preparation if they want that anointing and if they want to see a multiplication return in their lives.

The second parable in Matthew 25 is the parable of the talents. Here the master gave five talents, two talents, and one talent to three different servants. A talent was equivalent to $1,000 in today's currency. In this parable, hoarding was punished, but investing and trading produced a 100 per cent return for the two faithful servants. This parable speaks to the sowing and reaping of all that God puts in our hands in terms of money and abilities.

> *"... Jesus wants us to care for the sick, the hungry, the hurting, the naked, and the prisoners, and to invest time, money, and resources into these people."*

Finally, there is the parable of the sheep and the goats. Jesus taught that every believer will be judged on how they treat other believers. Even more convicting is the statement by Christ that whatever we do to the least of His brethren, we do it to Him. In this parable, the Lord expects us to invest in the needs of others. He wants us to be like the Good Samaritan, who took the poor man beaten up by thieves to an inn and accepted financial responsibility for him until he was healed and mended. Jesus wants us to care for the sick, the hungry, the hurting, the naked, and the prisoners, and to invest time, money, and resources into these people.

Sowing and Reaping for Multiplication Returns

With Matthew 25 as a background, lets look at the key Scripture for this chapter from 2 Corinthians.

But this I say: "He who sows sparingly will also reap sparingly, and he who sows bountifully will also reap bountifully. So let each one give as he purposes in his heart, not grudgingly or of necessity; for God loves a cheerful giver. And God is able to

make all grace abound toward you, that you, always having all sufficiency in all things, may have an abundance for every good work. As it is written: 'He has dispersed abroad, He has given to the poor; His righteousness endures forever.' Now may He who supplies seed to the sower, and bread for food, supply and **multiply** *the seed you have sown and increase the fruits of your righteousness, while you are enriched in everything for all liberality, which causes thanksgiving through us to God.*
2 Corinthians 9:6-11 *(emphasis added)*

God does not give us money, time, talents, and resources to hoard. We must invest into others and especially into God's family if we want God to multiply our seed and bring us a harvest. I am not talking about a "name it and claim it" Gospel, where the focus is on getting. We must set our hearts on fulfilling the Great Commission and sowing into the Lord's harvest.

> *"... God does not give us money, time, talents, and resources to hoard. We must invest into others and especially into God's family"*

When we began the video recordings for our ISOM Bible school program, we had very little money. My wife and I, with our two small children, had been on the mission field in Nigeria. We returned to the United States with five suitcases and a vision from God to create a video Bible school that could be translated into any language on earth. It was a huge task and we had very little financial support.

An early part of my vision was to do the live recordings simultaneously in fourteen languages. Logistically, this required fourteen isolation booths, which at the time cost about $36,000. I ordered those booths in faith, not having a clue as to how I was going to pay for them. God supernaturally provided the down payment of $17,000, leaving a balance of close to $19,000. The booths took about four months to make. About two weeks before our recordings started, the booths were ready, but the balance had to be paid before they would ship them to us.

We had almost no money in the bank at the time, and I did not want to impose that huge expense on any of my friends. As I desperately searched for some way to get those booths shipped to us in time for our first recordings, I remembered that I had been offered a platinum credit card from American Express while I was in Nigeria. There was no spending limit on it but payment in full was required by the next billing cycle.

With great trepidation, I charged those isolation booths to my AMEX card. My wife was terrified, and I must make it clear that I never recommend foolish credit decisions to any of my students. Where I was at that time, I had no other options. Then I prayed, *Lord, I'm not getting these translation booths for my own use. You know they are to help reach nations with Your truth. Lord, each booth represents a language group for whom Jesus died. Either You are with me in this, or You are not, and if You are not with me, I want to find out now because I don't want to go any further with this huge venture by myself.*

God did wonderfully supply the funds for those booths and that step of faith launched my wife and I on a financial journey of faith that has not stopped until this day. Month after month, we continue to step out on the supernatural waters of trusting God for huge amounts of money. To the glory of God, our ministry has never missed a payroll and, to date, we have paid all our bills on time. In addition, we now sow money to help others in distant lands, and God is always faithful to supply our needs. I know God holds us up because our hearts are set on the harvest, on reaching the unreached, and on making the Word of God known to people in their mother tongues.

Living to Give

Giving into the end-time harvest unlocks multiplication financial blessings into the hand of the sower. When we recorded our ISOM curriculum, we used a veteran missionary from Mexico named Wayne Meyers to teach on the subject of finances. The title of his course was "Living to Give." This man had been used by God to give away more cars to pastors in Mexico than anyone I know. He also has helped provide roofs to dozens of churches across Mexico. Wayne and his wife, Martha, live simply, using their faith to provide finances to the poor. Wayne is so loved by pastors in Mexico that a few years ago, when he had to undergo open-heart surgery, Mexican pastors crossed the border and paid his $60,000 hospital bill in cash. They had learned about giving from their mentor.

One thing that always struck me about Wayne was his face. It glowed like the sun and emanated such wonderful joy. I remember offering up this prayer: *Lord, if giving brings about that much joy, teach me to be a giver.*

I am not the only one who was bitten by the giving bug through Wayne Myers. In 1988, a coworker of mine named Grant Gill drove Wayne on a speaking tour around England. He was amazed by Wayne's stories of giving cars away to pastors. As he meditated on Wayne's testimonies about how God supernaturally provided resources for those vehicles, Grant began to wonder if he too could be used by God to help provide needed transportation to pastors on the mission field.

The next time Grant visited Africa, he had a burning desire to bless less-fortunate people. He believed God would help him if he could only maintain a right disposition of heart. While driving down the road of an African town, he noticed a large sign that read, "Car Auction Today." He felt a strong prompting to pull into the parking lot.

The auction, which had just begun, was being conducted through a silent bidding process. Grant put extremely low bids on all eleven cars being auctioned, hoping he would at least win one of the bids because he had a small sum of money with him and could only afford one. When the envelopes were opened, Grant was shocked to discover that he had won all eleven bids. Now he began to sweat because the sealed bids were legal and binding and he did not have the funds to pay for all of those cars.

Grant prayed a quick prayer for God's direction. As a stalling measure he asked the auctioneer if he could test-drive the best of the vehicles he had just purchased. The auctioneer obliged and gave him the keys to a late model green Ford Sierra. He drove away desperately seeking wisdom from God.

As Grant drove that sedan down the street, he noticed a large Ford dealership sign with the words, "We buy used Fords for CASH." Grant felt prompted to go in and see if he could sell the car he had just bought. The used-car dealer looked the car over, and astonished Grant by offering him not only enough to pay the Sierra off, but enough to pay off all eleven cars.

Grant sold that one Sierra to the Ford dealership and was able to give the other ten cars away. That miraculous experience launched Grant on a quest to give more cars away to missionaries and needy people. At the point of writing this book, he had given a total of thirty cars away and had car thirty-one in waiting to be sown where the Lord would direct.

This true story illustrates how God will give seed to the sower. If we set our hearts on giving into the gospel, with no other agenda, God will put seed in our hands and then multiply that seed. Let's look once again at the portion of Scripture with which we started.

*Now may He who supplies seed to the sower, and bread for food, supply and **multiply** the seed you have sown and increase the fruits of your righteousness, while you are enriched in everything*

for all liberality, which causes thanksgiving through us to God.
2 Corinthians 9:10-11 *(emphasis added)*

Sowing as a Sacrifice

Money is just one area God will multiply in fulfillment of the Abraham promise. As we set our hearts on giving selflessly of our time, our money, our prayers, and our resources to bless others, we will see this same multiplication principle manifest itself. When that little boy in the bible gave his bread and fish to Jesus, he had no idea of the multiplication that would result. (Matthew chapter 14) He only knew that he was giving up the little he had and probably thought he would go hungry that day.

What unlocks this multiplication principle is more an unselfish attitude of heart than a formula. There is also a strong connection between sacrifice and multiplication.

> *"... Multiplication is birthed out of obedient sacrifice."*

Think of it; the Abraham promise was given as the result of Abraham being willing to sacrifice Isaac, his most valuable asset, in consecrated obedience to God. Multiplication is birthed out of obedient sacrifice.

The greater our willingness to obey and sacrifice, the greater God's release of multiplication growth. Jesus' sacrifice on the cross is the highest fulfillment of this principle. In Him, all the nations of the earth are blessed because He sacrificed His very life. He was heaven's greatest treasure but the Father willingly sacrificed Him for our salvation. Is this not what John 3:16 is all about?

*For God so loved the world that He **gave** His only begotten Son, that whoever believes in Him should not perish but have everlasting life. **John 3:16** (emphasis added)*

We may not have much, but if we are willing to sacrifice what we have, putting it in the Master's Hands, He will multiply our seed and feed a multitude. We simply need to ensure our motivation is love, and that we give, like God did, so that people can believe in Jesus and not perish but have everlasting life. We can also be assured that our giving will personally bless us because, as Jesus pointed out, "It is more blessed to give than to receive." (Acts 20:35)

Chapter 15
Multiplication Through Unity

Key #7 – God Will Multiply Our Efforts Through Agreement

The final area that God will multiply if His people do their part involves unity. This is a principle that goes all the way back to the book of Genesis. When the whole earth had one language and were unified in building the tower of Babel, God said the following about mankind.

And the Lord said, "Indeed the people are one and they all have one language, and this is what they begin to do; now nothing that they propose to do will be withheld from them."
Genesis 11:6

God recognized the incredible potential for evil that existed if people simply became unified in their purpose. This was the reason God created divisions through language barriers.

The same idea of unlimited potential through unity can apply to God's people for good. Even in the natural there is an amazing principle called synergy. For example, I heard about a Canadian competition in which huge Clydesdale horses were hitched to a special sled that allows weights to be added to measure the horse's strength. During one competition, the winning horse pulled about 8,000 pounds, while the second-place finisher pulled 7,000 pounds.

The competition also included a team-pulling event, and it turned out that one of the teams consisted of the first- and second-place finishers from the individual pulling event. Logically, together they should be able to pull about 15,000 pounds. But because of the principle of synergy, when the two horses were hitched together, they managed to pull a sled weighing over 33,000 pounds, more than double the total amount they were able to pull individually.

Consider the following promise that Jesus gave.

Again I say to you that if two of you agree on earth concerning anything that they ask, it will be done for them by My Father in heaven. For where two or three are gathered together in My name, I am there in the midst of them." **Matthew 18:19-20**

Where two or three believers gather in unity, Jesus made it clear that another dimension would be added that would multiply the impact of the two individual believers. He promised to manifest Himself with all His resources in their midst.

Unity of the Faith

There are three main elements involved in bringing about such a unity. The first involves a unity of the faith or being in fundamental agreement concerning one's understanding of God's Word. When two or more believers are walking in obedience to the dictates of Scripture, then there is a unity of doctrine and a unity of understanding in the things of God. The promise of multiplied strength through obedience to God's commandments is one that goes back to the days of Moses.

> *"... Where two or three believers gather in unity, Jesus made it clear that another dimension would be added that would multiply the impact of the two individual believers."*

*If you walk in My statutes and keep My commandments, and perform them, then I will give you rain in its season, the land shall yield its produce, and the trees of the field shall yield their fruit... You will chase your enemies, and they shall fall by the sword before you. **Five of you shall chase a hundred, and a hundred of you shall put ten thousand to flight; your enemies shall fall by the sword before you.** For I will look on you favorably and make you fruitful, multiply you and confirm My covenant with you.*
***Leviticus 26:3-4, 7-9** (emphasis added)*

This is one reason why Paul labored so hard in teaching God's people sound doctrine. Peter also warned about others coming in with damnable heresies.

But there were also false prophets among the people, even as there will be false teachers among you, who will secretly bring in destructive heresies, even denying the Lord who bought them, and bring on themselves swift destruction.
2 Peter 2:1

There is a huge need in the body of Christ for good teaching because false doctrine opens the door for heresy and demonic influence. Wrong teaching also creates division in the church and hinders the unity of God's people. When unity is undermined, then God's ability to move in power among His people is seriously affected.

There is a balance to this need for solid doctrine and a unity of understanding concerning the Scriptures. Some believers become so bogged down in minute interpretations of certain Bible verses that they are never able to come into agreement with other brothers and sisters in Christ. Paul gave the following warning to Timothy concerning his church members.

Remind them of these things, charging them before the Lord not to strive about words to no profit, to the ruin of the hearers.
2 Timothy 2:14

It is possible for believers to ruin themselves and others over their view of the end times or over the Bible's teaching about how a Sabbath should be observed. There are many areas in Scripture that are mysteries and there are other areas where believers hold differing positions but all out of a good conscience. We are told to respect the conscience of others even if we don't exactly see it their way. Here is what Paul wrote about eating meat.

Receive one who is weak in the faith, but not to disputes over doubtful things. For one believes he may eat all things, but he who is weak eats only vegetables. Let not him who eats despise him who does not eat, and let not him who does not eat judge him who eats; for God has received him. **Romans 14:1-3**

I think the slogan adopted by the Evangelical Presbyterian Church (EPC) denomination bears repeating and is worth living by[18].

> In essentials, unity; in non-essentials, liberty;
> in all things charity.

Unity of Community

Unity of doctrine is one foundation but there must be more. There must also be a unity of community. There are many facets to this kind of unity but I want to highlight four that are clearly shown in the book of Acts. These are prayer, identity, purpose and love. The first real glimpse into the unified early church community was in the upper room on the day of Pentecost.

When the Day of Pentecost had fully come, they were all with one accord in one place. And suddenly there came a sound from heaven, as of a rushing mighty wind, and it filled the whole house where they were sitting. Then there appeared to them divided tongues, as of fire, and one sat upon each of them. And they were all filled with the Holy Spirit and began to speak with other tongues, as the Spirit gave them utterance. **Acts 2:1-4**

These one hundred and twenty believers had a strong sense of family and a common identity with Christ and each other. They were praying together when the Holy Spirit was poured out from God. Most of them had seen the risen Messiah and memories of their Master's words and deeds were fresh in their minds. They also knew they were under assault from hostile leaders who had recently crucified their Lord.

It was into this atmosphere of agreement that God was able to manifest His power. A few chapters later, we see a massive persecution arise against the saints of God. As in war, troops unify against a common enemy and this attack brought the early church together in prayer.

*And being let go, they went to their own companions and reported all that the chief priests and elders had said to them. So when they heard that, they raised their voice to God with **one accord** and said: "Lord, You are God, who made heaven and earth and the sea, and all that is in them... Now, Lord, look on their threats, and grant to Your servants that with all boldness they may speak Your word, by stretching out Your hand to heal, and that signs and wonders may be done through the name of Your holy Servant Jesus." And when they had prayed, the place where they were assembled together was shaken; and they were all filled with the Holy Spirit, and they spoke the word of God with boldness. Now the multitude of those who believed were of **one heart and one soul**; neither did anyone say that any of the things he possessed was his own, but they had all things in common.*
Acts 4:23-24, 29-32 *(emphasis added)*

In this Scripture, we can see all four aspects of a unified community. Firstly, the believers lifted their voices together and prayed. Secondly, they had a purpose in their prayer and that was evangelism. They asked for boldness to speak the message of the gospel and for signs and wonders to confirm their evangelism efforts. Thirdly, there was a strong identification with Jesus and His people. They knew they were being persecuted not for their own sakes but because they represented Christ and His message on the earth. This sense of identity was so strong that it led to the fourth element of the community, which was love. So strong was the bond between them that they shared everything. Jesus manifested Himself right in their midst and His power was released among them.

I have been deeply moved by the words of professor Gilbert Bilezikian. He was a mentor of Bill Hybels and was the one who inspired his vision of local churches becoming Acts 4 communities. He described those early church believers as being "radically devoted to God and to each other, relentless in their pursuit of people

> "... The devil has one major objective, to keep believers from uniting their prayers and their warfare against him. He would far rather that believers focus their energies fighting each other."

outside the community, free with their worship, active with their servanthood, transformational with their teaching, expectant with their prayers and outrageous with their generosity.[19]"

I believe it is the cry of God's heart for the body of Christ to return to the kind of unity found in that fourth chapter of Acts. Because unity in prayer, purpose identity and love are so critical, we can understand some of the devil's strategies to stop these kinds of agreement at all costs. Satan does it through stirring up unforgiveness, selfishness, jealousy, strife, gossip, hatred, lies and through encouraging every work of the flesh. The devil has one major objective, to keep believers from uniting their prayers and their warfare against him. He would far rather that believers focus their energies fighting each other.

As we think about all the factions and schisms in the body of Christ, we can see the devil being very successful at dividing God's people. I believe this is soon going to change as believers start understanding who they are in Jesus, who they belong to, and who their enemy really is.

Unity under Authority

The last area that affects unity involves leadership and authority. The original disunity in heaven was the result of Lucifer rebelling against God's rule. Unfortunately, a similar situation results today whenever people violate God ordained lines of authority.

> *"... The anointing of God always flows from leadership to the people under them."*

This type of rebellion may happen between a wife and a husband, between children and parents, between God's saints and church leadership, between an employee and a boss, or in a nation between people and their government. Just like in an army, when chains of command are violated, confusion and strife result.

The anointing of God always flows from leadership to the people under them. As leaders fear God and walk in integrity, those under them will be blessed. This is especially true as all people under leadership yield to the authority God places over their lives. Consider the following Psalm of David.

Behold, how good and how pleasant it is For brethren to dwell together in unity! It is like the precious oil upon the head, Running down on the beard, The beard of Aaron, Running down on the edge of his garments. It is like the dew of Hermon, Descending upon the mountains of Zion; For there the Lord commanded the blessing— Life forevermore. **Psalm 133:1-3**

We see in this powerful Psalm the principle of unity being equated to precious oil that flows from the head to the beard and down to the edge of the garments. As believers dwell together in unity, as they flow with God's lines of authority, then God's anointing oil is able to reach them and God's blessing will be commanded upon their lives.

When churches facilitate a unity of the faith, a unity of community and a unity under authority among their members, then Satan is in serious trouble. This is because man's part gets fulfilled and God's multiplication promise of blessing will begin to manifest. Those churches will then see a massive increase of God's power among them and they will experience the presence of Jesus in a wonderful new way.

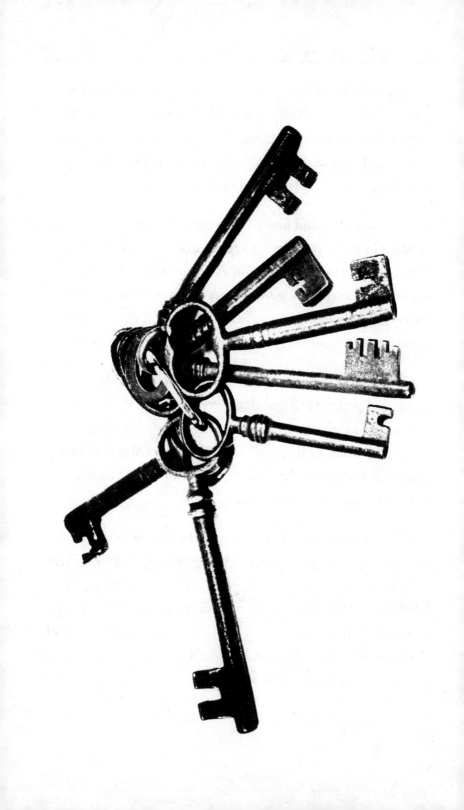

Chapter 16
Human Multiplication Vehicles

The main focus of this book has been on human functions that God will multiply. God has also given mankind the ability to multiply through human efforts. Man has done a great job at multiplying everything from Coca Cola to cars, from apple trees to airplanes, from hats to hamburgers. Going back to the beginning, God gave Adam and Eve this command.

"Be fruitful and multiply; fill the earth and subdue it; have dominion over the fish of the sea, over the birds of the air, and over every living thing that moves on the earth."
Genesis 1:27-28

As I mentioned in chapter 3, this is one of the very few commands that mankind has been faithful to obey. The point I really want to drive home is that the responsibility to multiply was placed firmly on the shoulders of Adam and Eve. Extending this concept, we can conclude that God has placed within people a huge potential to fill the earth with all kinds of things through human multiplication efforts.

A Dynamic Partnership

When it comes to building God's Kingdom, there is a great partnership between human multiplication efforts and God's divine impartations. We can learn much about this principle from a short story in 2 Kings chapter 4.

A certain woman of the wives of the sons of the prophets cried out to Elisha, saying, "Your servant my husband is dead, and you know that your servant feared the Lord. And the creditor is coming to take my two sons to be his slaves." So Elisha said to her, "What shall I do for you? Tell me, what do you have in the house?" And she said, "Your maidservant has nothing in the house but a jar of oil." Then he said, "Go, borrow vessels from everywhere, from all your neighbors—empty vessels; do not gather just a few. And when you have come in, you shall shut the door behind you and your sons; then pour it into all those vessels, and set aside the full ones." So she went from him and shut the door behind her and her sons, who brought the vessels to her; and she poured it out. Now it came to pass, when the vessels were full, that she said to her son, "Bring me another vessel." And he said to her, "There is not another vessel." So the oil ceased. Then she came and told the man of God. And he said, "Go, sell the oil and pay your debt; and you and your sons live on the rest." 2 Kings 4:1-7

This story reveals a powerful dynamic between the human effort of the widow and her sons and the degree of multiplication by God. Had the poor widow and her sons been able to get 200 massive empty drums, I believe the multiplication of God would have filled them all. If they had built a factory to manufacture drums for oil, I believe God would have filled them all as well. What we see from this account is that God's multiplication of the oil was limited by the human ability of the family to gather tangible vessels to carry the oil. When there were no more vessels, the miracle stopped.

> *"... Had the poor widow and her sons been able to get 200 massive empty drums, I believe the multiplication of God would have filled them all."*

Natural Construction that Releases Spiritual Glory

Could it be that man can limit God's anointing from filling vessels by simply not providing God with enough vessels to fill? Are not churches tangible vessels that God can fill with His anointing? How about cell groups, schools for children, universities, orphanages, elderly care homes, and Bible training centers? Are they not all vessels that God can fill if we will simply establish them or construct them? Only as man builds such tangible vessels can God fill them with His anointing and they can become conduits of His blessings.

Think of it, the early apostles turned their whole world upside down in a single generation. They brought the Gospel from what is now Spain in the west to India in the east. They were driven with such zeal and passion that they would stop at nothing to achieve world evangelization. Their strategy was to establish local churches in every city they visited. These congregations became vehicles of God's blessing into each region. From the book of Revelation, we see that Jesus

> *"... Could it be that man can limit God's anointing from filling vessels by simply not providing God with enough vessels to fill?"*

Himself saw each local church as an oil-containing candlestick. (Revelation 1:20)

There was a natural side to the establishment of each local church and a spiritual side. Jesus made it clear that the spiritual aspect of each church had to be maintained or else He would remove His candlestick from that church, cut off the conduit of divine oil, and leave only a human shell behind that would soon die. (Revelation 2:5) Local churches today need to be built naturally, but more importantly they need to be built spiritually according to the pattern revealed in the New Testament. Paul spoke of himself as a wise master builder.

For we are God's fellow workers; you are God's field, you are God's building. According to the grace of God which was given to me, as a wise master builder I have laid the foundation, and another builds on it. But let each one take heed how he builds on it. For no other foundation can anyone lay than that which is laid, which is Jesus Christ. Now if anyone builds on this foundation with gold, silver, precious stones, wood, hay, straw, each one's work will become clear; for the Day will *declare it, because it will be revealed by fire; and the fire will test each one's work, of what sort it is. **1 Corinthians 3:9-13***

We see this principle both with Moses constructing a tabernacle in the wilderness and with Solomon when he built the temple. Each had to painstakingly build a natural edifice according to a prescribed pattern. At the point of completion of the natural, this is what happened.

*And he (Moses) raised up the court all around the tabernacle and the altar, and hung up the screen of the court gate. So Moses finished the work. Then the cloud covered the tabernacle of meeting, and the glory of the Lord filled the tabernacle. And Moses was not able to enter the tabernacle of meeting, because the cloud rested above it, and the glory of the Lord filled the tabernacle. **Exodus 40:33-35***

*When Solomon had finished praying, fire came down from heaven and consumed the burnt offering and the sacrifices; and the glory of the Lord filled the temple. And the priests could not enter the house of the Lord, because the glory of the Lord had filled the Lord's house. **2 Chronicles 7:1&2***

At the point of completing the natural construction, we see God filling both Old Testament meeting places with His glory. It was important with Solomon and with Moses that these places were built very carefully according to a heavenly pattern.

If New Testament churches today are built in a right way, God will fill them with His glory. The natural human side of each church plant in the book of Acts was no easy process. Most new

churches were birthed amidst massive persecution. The Apostle
Paul paid for each of his church plants with stonings, beatings,
imprisonments, and often treacherous
conditions. He then spent the rest of
his life nurturing those church plants
to maturity. Co-working with God in the natural is difficult, but people have to
prepare churches, cell groups, Bible training centers, schools,
universities, orphanages, and other kinds of vehicles in increasing
numbers for God to fill with his glory and to become conduits of
God's anointing and blessing into the lives of people.

> *"... The Apostle Paul paid for each of his church plants with stonings, beatings, imprisonments, and often treacherous conditions."*

Media Multiplication

This brings me to the greatest vessel our generation has been
given to carry God's anointing to the uttermost parts of the
earth, and that is media.

The following statement was made about the early apostles
and church leaders.

"If they did what they did with what they had,
    imagine what we could do with what we have,
        if we had what they had."

Source Unknown

We need the zeal of the early church, their passion to establish godly churches and modern technology to help us get the job done. It is my conviction that the hi-tech tools of our day have been given to the world primarily to help fulfill the Great Commission. Technology is the closest practical gift to our generation of what Jesus did with the loaves and the fishes. Jesus broke them and fed a multitude. Now, it is not natural bread that can be multiplied, it is spiritual bread.

> *"... We can feed millions with God's Word through technology and Jesus has given us the ability to multiply that life giving food."*

We can feed millions with God's Word through technology and Jesus has given us the ability to multiply that life giving food. Once again we have a natural responsibility to create and duplicate tangible materials that are able to carry the anointing of God to others.

When visiting Tulsa, Oklahoma, I visited a museum that honored mission works and missionaries from the past. Prominent in the museum was a copy of the Gutenberg Bible and the Gutenberg press. What gripped my heart was a statement written by Johan Gutenberg in the 1450's when he was contemplating the awesome implications for the Gospel of his new invention. He wrote.

"Yes, it is a press, certainly, but a press from which shall soon flow, in inexhaustible streams, the most abundant and marvelous liquor that has ever flowed to relieve the thirst of

men! Through it God will spread His Word. A spring of pure truth shall flow from it; like a new star it shall scatter the darkness of ignorance, and cause a light heretofore unknown to shine amongst men."

In 1999, CNN did a countdown series of the hundred most significant inventions of the past 1,000 years. With all the leaps in science, engineering, medicine, and technology, the number-one position went to Johan Gutenberg and his invention of the printing press.

When I consider the technology of our day, I am gripped by a sense of awe and excitement at the potential we have at our disposal. Through technology, we can dispel ignorance in our world and cause God's light to shine into places that presently lie in darkness. Our message is urgently needed and the souls of millions hang in the balance.

Vessels Queen Esther Used to Save Israel

During the days of Queen Esther the Jews in 127 provinces were under a decree of death issued, under the king's authority, from an evil man named Haman. The king's order could not be altered, but there was one way of escape. As the day of death approached, Queen Esther and her uncle, Mordecai, had to move quickly to get a message of deliverance to Jews dwelling throughout the Persian Empire. Here is how it happened.

So the king's scribes were called at that time, in the third month, which is the month of Sivan, on the twenty-third day; and it was written, according to all that Mordecai commanded, to the

*Jews, the satraps, the governors, and the princes of the provinces from India to Ethiopia, one hundred and twenty-seven provinces in all, **to every province in its own script, to every people in their own language**, and to the Jews in their **own script and language**. And he wrote in the name of king Ahasuerus, sealed it with the king's signet ring, and sent letters by couriers on horseback, riding on royal horses bred from **swift steeds**. By these letters the king permitted the Jews who were in every city to gather together and protect their lives, to destroy, kill and annihilate all the forces of any people or province that would assault them, both little children and women, and to plunder their possessions...A copy of the document was to be issued as a decree in every province and **published for all people**, so that the Jews would be ready on that day to avenge themselves on their enemies. The couriers who rode on royal horses went out, hastened and pressed on by the king's command.*
***Esther 8:9-11, 13-14** (emphasis added)*

This is a picture of what the church of Jesus Christ needs to be doing today. Without Christ, there is a death sentence over all humanity. We have a message of escape that will bring deliverance from death. This message must get out. As in the days of Queen Esther, the message still needs to be put into the languages of the nations so it will be understood in every province and country of our world.

Esther used the quickest means of delivery of her day, which was horseback, to distribute a hand-copied decree. We have a faster means of delivery through the steeds of media and technology. These are the horses of the twenty-first century, which can carry the message to all the provinces. The day of death is fast approaching. May we be gripped with the same sense of urgency that motivated Esther and Mordecai. They saved all the Jews of their day. Through our message and means of delivery, we too can save nations.

> *"... Esther used the quickest means of delivery of her day, which was horseback, to distribute a hand-copied decree. We have a faster means of delivery through the steeds of media and technology. These are the horses of the twenty-first century"*

I believe it is in the heart of God to use technology to equip an end-time spiritual army. Jesus looked on the harvest with compassion and told His disciples to pray that He would send laborers into His harvest. There is no army without recruitment and without training. We must use technology to prepare laborers to take the message of Christ's love into the dark regions of the earth. Caution, however, must be taken not to undermine local church leadership by divorcing teaching and training from the life of each local congregation. Construction must always be according to the heavenly pattern.

In this hour of history, the church must tap into as many electronic delivery systems as possible. With the release to the world of Mel Gibson's *The Passion of the Christ*, the global church has been given an incredible insight into the power of media to reach people for Jesus. Perhaps more unsaved people had an encounter with the gospel in the first two months of that movie than through almost any other evangelistic effort of our time or any time in history.

The Scriptures clearly reveal that in the end times, the gospel will be preached to every tribe, nation tongue and people (Revelation 14:6). God is going to confront every person with the message of Jesus before the end comes. The question is whether the body of Christ will be ready to disciple and shepherd the massive wave of impacted people who decide they want to follow the Master.

I encourage all ministries, denominations, movements and individuals to develop tangible tools for the tasks of discipleship and leadership training. I also urge them to aggressively produce and create the vessels through which God's Kingdom can be built. Humanity hangs in the balance, the body of Christ has the answers and an urgent task needs to be accomplished for the sake of Calvary.

> *"... Strategies that only add leaders, disciples and churches will not be sufficient in this hour. Those ways of doing things must step aside so that God's multiplication strategies can come to the forefront and be fully implemented."*

Strategies that only add leaders, disciples and churches will not be sufficient in this hour. Those ways of doing things must step aside so that God's multiplication strategies can come to the forefront and be fully implemented. We must put off the old wineskins and embrace the new. As the human and the divine work together, God will not be limited, nations will be reached, and the Abraham promise will be unlocked.

Conclusion

My vision for the future is for every church to become a place where God's people are trained, equipped, discipled, and released. God has already put five-fold ministry abilities and kingdom-building giftings into churches all over the world. As pastors equip their saints, using mature leaders to do the teaching, people will rise up to a place of fruitfulness in their churches. From these people, Jesus will anoint and call multitudes of laborers and send them forth into His harvest field of the world. This army of trained believers will reap the harvest and establish new churches, which will care for the new lambs and begin the process all over again.

If we do our part, and let God do the multiplying, we can get the job done. It is His will, and He is showing us His way.

I close this book by leaving you with a prophetic Scripture that has become a pillar in our ministry. It is from the book of Daniel, and its context is the end times. Specifically it refers to the abomination of desolation. Jesus made reference to this in the Gospel of Matthew.

Therefore when you see the abomination of desolation, spoken of by Daniel the prophet, standing in the holy place (whoever reads, let him understand. **Matthew 24:15**

For then there will be great tribulation, such as has not been since the beginning of the world until this time, no, nor ever shall be. **Matthew 24:21**

The following Scripture from the book of Daniel pertains to the end times, and most bible scholars are convinced we are very close to those days. This Scripture also refers to a figure in end-time prophecy most often identified as the Antichrist. With that as a backdrop, let's look at the following prophetic verses:

*And forces shall be mustered by him (the antichrist), and they shall defile the sanctuary fortress; then they shall take away the daily sacrifices, and place there the abomination of desolation. Those who do wickedly against the covenant he shall corrupt with flattery; but the people who know their God shall be strong and carry out great exploits. And those of the people who **understand** shall **instruct many**... Daniel 11:31-33 (emphasis added)*

This Scripture most likely refers to our generation. In these end times, there will be a mass instruction of God's saints by people of understanding. The result will be believers who know their God and do great exploits. I believe this equipping of an end-time spiritual army is the next major item on God's agenda for the church. The preparation of this army will spearhead an unlocking of the Abraham promise.

It is time for the church to take the steps needed to unlock the Abraham promise. Christians must now step out to multiply the vessels and to do those things God has promised to multiply.

Praying the Abraham Promise

Lord, I thank You that I am the seed of Abraham because I belong to Christ Jesus. I am therefore an heir of the promise that You swore to Abraham. I ask that blessing You will bless me, and multiplying, You will multiply me as the stars in the heaven and the sand on the seashore. I ask that I will possess the gate of my enemies, and that through Christ in me, all the nations of the earth will be blessed.

Artwork and Design

Front: Photograph of Vatican Library door: José A. Warletta
Back: Photograph of passage way: Michal Charko
Cover and Design: James Kallas — isom.org
Special Thanks to Paul Limon for help with the lock

End Notes

[1] Brown, Driver, Briggs and Gesenius. "Hebrew Lexicon entry for Zera`". "The KJV Old Testament Hebrew Lexicon". <http://www.biblestudytools.net/Lexicons/Hebrew/heb.cgi?number=2233&version=kjv>.

Strong's Concordance # 02233 ,
 (World Bible Publishers, Iowa Falls,1986)

2 Australian National Reporter - ANU Reporter, 2003 – August Edition http://info.anu.edu.au/mac/Newsletters_and_Journals/ANU_Reporter/August%202003.asp

[3] Spirit Filled Life Bible, (Thomas Nelson, Inc. 1991) p. 656

[4] Author Unknown

5 Newsletter - (Reproduced by kind permission of David G. Hathaway, www.propheticvision.org.uk)

[6] God's Story Project - http://www.gods-story.org – Hemet, CA

[7] Many Internet locations – original source unknown

[8] Thayer and Smith. "Greek Lexicon entry for Tereo". "The KJV New Testament Greek Lexicon". <http://www.biblestudytools.net/Lexicons/Greek/grk.cgi?number=5083&version=kjv>.

Strong's Concordance # 5083 ,
 (World Bible Publishers, Iowa Falls,1986)

[9] Thayer and Smith. "Greek Lexicon entry for Dialegomai". "The KJV New Testament Greek Lexicon". Strong's # 1256, ibid <http://www.biblestudytools.net/Lexicons/Greek/grk.cgi?number=1256&version=kjv>

[10] Thayer and Smith. "Greek Lexicon entry for Peitho". "The KJV New Testament Greek Lexicon". Strong's # 3982, ibid <http://www.biblestudytools.net/Lexicons/Greek/grk.cgi?number=3982&version=kjv>

[11] Ken Kesey – Comment made in an interview - Cited by Rawlins (1992)

[12] Numerous places on the Internet – Author unknown

[13] C. Peter Wagner, New Apostolic Churches (Ventura, 1998) p. 73

[14] Powerhouse Publishing, PO Box 99, Fawnskin, CA 92333 (909) 866 3119 – www.powerhouspublishing.org

[15] Dawn 2000 – Seven Million Churches to Go video, DAWN Ministries, Colorado Springs, 1992.

[16] Jim Feeney, The Team Method of Church Planting (Anchorage, Alaska, 1988) – Reprinted by permission 2000 by Good Shepherd Ministries Intl. (1-800 901 8175) www.jimfeeney.org

17 Ray Comfort, Revival's Golden Key (Gainesville, Florida, 2002), p. 68

[18] Evangelical Presbyterian Churches (EPC) – www.epc.org

[19] C. Peter Wagner, New Apostolic Churches (Ventura, 1998) p. 76

About the Author

Berin Gilfillan was born and raised in South Africa. He holds an undergraduate degree from the University of Michigan, a Master's degree in Communication from Regent University (formerly CBN University), and a Doctor of Ministry Degree from Vision International University. Berin also studied missions and church planting

Dr. Berin Gilfillan

for two years at Fuller Theological Seminary. In 1985, Berin married his wife, Lisa, and they have three children. Lisa works alongside Berin in the ministry, spearheading a training program for women called Women of the World (WOW).

Berin and Lisa worked from 1986-9 with the ministry of German evangelist Reinhard Bonnke. Berin headed up Bonnke's television ministry and Lisa headed up the publications department of that work. In 1991, they started the missionary ministry of Good Shepherd Ministries, International. From 1992-4, the Gilfillan family were missionaries in the country of Nigeria. There they started 140 video Bible schools and also pioneered a successful preschool.

Since 1994, Good Shepherd Ministries, International has been developing the International School of Ministry (ISOM), a project sometimes referred to as "the training equivalent of the *Jesus* movie". The ISOM consists of video training material that easily can be translated into any language on earth. The purpose of the ISOM is to disciple people and to train leaders on a massive scale. Teachers who have recorded for the program include Joyce Meyer, Reinhard Bonnke, Marilyn Hickey, John Bevere, Jack Hayford, Dick Eastman, T.L Osborn and about 25 other well-known Christian ministers. Dr. T.L. Osborn said, concerning the ISOM: "As far as I know, the development of this Curriculum is the most important thing happening on the earth for the Kingdom of God today."

The ISOM curriculum currently is being used in 141 nations and in over 60 of the world's major languages. By 2006, at least 12,000 training sites around the world had been identified that were using ISOM materials. Berin's ministry combines a solid missions understanding with cutting edge technology to facilitate the training of church-planters, laborers and ministry leaders. He strongly endorses pastoral leadership and authority, and believes every local church should become a training center to equip God's people. He and his wife Lisa have recently produced a new curriculum to train and equip Women. That curriculum also uses very renowned teachers such as Joyce Meyer, Marilyn Hickey, Lisa Bevere, Bobby Houston and Darlene Zschech. In addition, Good Shepherd is partnering with Global Expeditors to produce dynamic material for local church youth groups. Current information about the ministry can be found at www.isom.org